Spiritual Cosmetics
for the Soul

(New Small Edition)

Perfecting Your Inner Beauty

Devotionals for
Men & Women

By
E.A. James

FM Publishing Company
Cherokee, NC 28719

Spiritual Cosmetics for the Soul

Perfecting Your Inner Beauty
Devotionals for Men & Women (New Small Edition)

Spiritual Cosmetics for the Soul

ISBN 9781931671552

Library of Congress Control Number 2013954593

Copyright © 2010 by Elizabeth Abigail James

FM Publishing Company

P.O. Box 215

Cherokee, NC 28719

Dedication

This book is dedicated first and foremost to my Father in Heaven who is always the head of my life, to my children and grandchildren. We, who are the older generation, must decrease while they must increase. They are my legacy. It is my prayer that they serve God for the rest of their days and worship him in Spirit and in Truth, so that *"when we all get to heaven, what a day of rejoicing that will be, when we all see Jesus, we will sing and shout the VICTORY!"*

God bless you.

E. A. James
A Servant of Christ

Introduction

Cosmetics are substances used to enhance the appearance or scent of the human body. They are also used for the purposes of cleansing, beautifying, promoting attractiveness or alternating one's appearance. Although we call them cosmetics when used by women and toiletries when used by men, they include skin-care creams, shaving creams, lotions, powders, shampoos, perfumes, lipsticks, nail polish, makeup, deodorant, permanent waves, colored contact lenses, hair colors, hair sprays, gels, and items for dental care. However, God is more concerned with our spiritual natures because these mortal bodies will one day put on immortality, and the corruptible will one day put on incorruptible. The Bible depicts us as the church, the bride of Christ who awaits the bridegroom. He is concerned with our spiritual nature. He is concerned with our soul. Can we be trusted with eternity is the question. To be presented in the Day of Judgment without spot, stain, or wrinkle, we need the cosmetic application of the Word of God. We need its life-giving water and blood as revealed in Christ Jesus to cover our confessed sins. We need it to rid ourselves of the terrible scent of sin. We need it for daily spiritual cleansing, beautifying, and for promoting our spiritual attractiveness. In other words, we need it to change us from glory to glory into the image of Christ. Our Lord and Savior is soon to return, and we need to be ready to receive him.

I know to say that this book is ordained by God sounds completely trite to most people, but it is the truth. I've written and published several books: poetry, songs, a novel, autobiographically-based nonfiction, and other nonfiction books. However, God put on my heart many years ago to write a devotional and I kept putting it off. It was not until a co-worker gave me a woman's devotional book published by LPM (Living Proof Ministries) called *New Every Morning*, that I was convicted again to obey God and write a book of devotionals. The *New Every Morning* book was written by Amanda Moore Jones and contains a compilation of her journal writings along with those of her mother. The devotionals truly touched my heart. The format for the prayer box and journal pages is fashioned after her book. The Small Edition does not contain the journal pages. Go to www.fmpublishingcompany.com to order the Journal Writing Edition.

Introduction (cont'd)

The content for the devotionals is from my own life and experiences and what God has revealed to me through his word. I have kept a prayer book and journal since 1995. The book contains over 800 names of people who were still living, and among the names on the list are businesses, organizations and groups. The prayers are petitions, requests, or intercessions for healing and/or salvation for me and for others. When prayers are answered or the person dies (unsaved) or goes to sleep in the Lord to await redemption (saved), I cross off their names and add a comment regarding the result of the prayer. What is amazing about the prayer book and journal is that although I've read through it several times, I did not have to consult its pages to write this book. I did, however, use past and present personal experiences, as the Lord led me, from the prayer book and journal. When we minister to anyone, the Word of God is incorporated into our lives first. It convicts us and changes us. Then and only then can we teach others and witness to the goodness of God. It does not mean we are completely healed and perfected; it just means we understand and recognize our weaknesses and our continual need for the Savior. God hears and answers our distress signal: S.O.S. (Save Our Souls!)

I have included one devotional for each week of the year. Each one is single-spaced and from 1-1/2 to 2 pages in length. Each one culminates with a prayer box to reinforce the message and to inspire commitment. I encourage you to use this section and allow God to minister to your hearts, so that you can be doers of the Word and not hearers only. In addition, an Alphabetic Index by Topic has been included at the end of the book in case devotional time by topic is your preference instead of chronologically by week. It is my earnest prayer that each one of these devotionals brings you conviction, peace, comfort, and knowledge that the Savior will help you through any trials or struggles in your lives.

Table of Contents

Week 1	Holding Out and Moving Ahead	8
Week 2	A Matter of Obedience	11
Week 3	A Test of Forgiveness	15
Week 4	Forgive Us Our Debts	19
Week 5	The Right to Choose Life	23
Week 6	Death Be Not Proud	27
Week 7	Can We Handle the Truth?	31
Week 8	Are We There Yet?	34
Week 9	Not Without My Armor	36
Week 10	Beyond My Foolishness	39
Week 11	Here I am, Send Me	42
Week 12	From Here to Eternity	45
Week 13	Joy Comes in the Morning	48
Week 14	The Best Grant of Immunity	54
Week 15	A Helpmate for All Seasons	57
Week 16	Those Are Fighting Words	61
Week 17	We Shall Overcome – Our Fear	64
Week 18	Show Them the Money	67
Week 19	Pulling Them Out of the Fire	71
Week 20	No More False Converts	74
Week 21	I Feel Therefore I Am	77
Week 22	Code of Conduct	80
Week 23	My Turn is Coming	82
Week 24	Timing is Everything	85
Week 25	Armed with Courage	88
Week 26	Avoiding the Extreme Makeover	91
Week 27	Going for the Gold or God	94
Week 28	The Right Path of Worship	97
Week 29	The Color of Lies	100

Table of Contents (cont'd)

Week 30   Fit as a Fiddle 103
Week 31   Taking Out the Garbage 106
Week 32   Always Room for One More 109
Week 33   Herein is Love 113
Week 34   Joy Comes After the Mourning.........................116
Week 35   A Position of Dignity......................................120
Week 36   Weak Ends, Power Begins.............................123
Week 37   Friend and Foe, Both I Know.........................128
Week 38   Our Vote of Confidence.................................132
Week 39   A Sickness Not Unto Death 135
Week 40   To Know Even As I Am Known.......................138
Week 41   True Fellowship 141
Week 42   The Greatest of Gifts 144
Week 43   Chasing the Wind...148
Week 44   Finishing the Race 152
Week 45   Unwelcomed Guests......................................155
Week 46   A Backsliding Atheist 159
Week 47   The Pursuit of Happiness...............................162
Week 48   Recognizing the Counterfeit 167
Week 49   Only One Way Up...171
Week 50   An Offer of a Lifetime 176
Week 51   Answering the Hard Questions of Our Faith
           (Part I) 180
Week 52   Answering the Hard Questions of Our Faith
           (Part II) 184

Alphabetical Index by Topic 188

About the Author..190

Book Ordering Information 194

Holding Out and Moving Ahead

"But without faith it is impossible to please him: for he that comes to God must believe that he is, and that he is a rewarder of them that diligently seek him." Hebrews 11:6

I've heard many people say that they don't have faith and don't believe in anything. In fact, they've tried to convince me that they are atheists. I don't buy it. I've watched them get into elevators, push a button, wait patiently for the doors to close, and faithfully trust it will take them where they want to go. I've watched them get on airplanes and faithfully trust that the pilot and the plane will get them to their destination. I know that before they go to sleep at night, they set their alarm clocks, close their eyes, and faithfully trust the alarm will awaken them the next day. So they do have faith: they trust in elevators, airplanes, and alarm clocks. However, what about faith and trust in God?

In September of 1996, I sent in my poem *Acquired Taste* to a national poetry convention located in California where the attendance cost would be $500 if they accepted my poem; however, they were giving away ten $1,000 prizes and one $5,000 prize. Without haste, I prayed and asked God for one of the $1,000 prizes. He revealed to me that he had one of them for me. They did accept my poem. It took a long time for me to get the $250 deposit and finally the remaining amount to attend the convention, but through the help of my mother, father, and friends, my daughter and I were driving to my mother's house in California where we would be staying for the two days.

We headed out at 4am in my 14-year-old dented, but paid for, Toyota. The enemy tried everything. He first went to work on my car. It overheated several times. We had to put water in the radiator, but had no more problems with it. This was very discouraging. I noticed that we had 109 miles to go to get to Blythe. I was tempted to turn back and just try and catch the bus. This would have depleted our funds even more. I decided to keep going.

8

When we got to Indio, I noticed the back tire was split at the top! It had a lot of tread still on it. I had a doughnut in the trunk, but only a piece of a jack. I prayed and decided to keep going. I drove the last 140 miles on that tire, praying all the way, and thanking God for every mile. My daughter knew I was getting tired, especially the last 50 miles, and she suggested that I stop and rest, but somehow I felt that if I could just hold out and keep moving ahead, the tire would hold out also. The song Bro. Otis sang in church *I've Got to Hold Out* kept ringing in my head. We made it to my mother's house. My mother, nor the tire repairman, could believe we drove that long on that tire! I used this as an opportunity to witness to the repairman and told him, "Let me tell you about a mighty God."

The enemy still didn't give up. He attacked my car on both Saturday and Sunday morning – the two days I had to drive to the poetry convention. My mom let me borrow her car both days. She also had her mechanic take a look at mine. On Saturday, the 300 poets, including me, listened as every contestant read or recited his or her poem. The poem I'd selected to recite was *Tears for Molly*. Each of the 300 poets voted for what they believed to be the best three. Each of us was to choose two other poems and could also vote for ourselves. A black woman told me that she had a dream where she saw me and several others, whom she pointed out, winning the prizes. I gratefully thanked her. However, there I sat. They'd called eight names and mine was not one of them. The enemy and his darts of doubt attacked me once again. He laughed and told me that I must feel really stupid because I'd driven all those miles in a raggedy car, took money from family and friends, probably ruined my car for good, and all for nothing, because I was not going to win. He said it was going to be a long ride on the road back home.

The Bible says that without faith it is impossible to please God and that he has no pleasure in those who turn back. The apostle Paul says that we are to forget those things that are behind and press toward the mark of the prize of the high calling in Christ Jesus. (Philippians 3:13-14) This is what I was determined to do. When you know God is behind you, before you, beneath you, above you, and on either side of you, it's easy to keep going and move forward. David, a man after God's own heart, said, "The LORD is my light and my salvation; whom shall I fear? The LORD is the strength of my life; of whom shall I be afraid?" (Psalm 27:1) With these words in mind, I said in my heart, "Get behind me Satan, the Lord rebuke you. God said it and I believe it." I was the next name they called.

I copied the $1,000 check and sent it the naysayers and keep it as a reminder of the faith and trust that it took for me to accomplish something amazing, not of my own power, but through the mighty power of God's grace and mercy.

> God forgive me when I doubt your power and your Word. Open up my spiritual eyes and ears to see the wonderful gifts and surprises you have in store for me each day. May I always use your talents and gifts for your service and glory, and let prayer and your Word lead me daily into ever increasing faith. Amen

A Matter of Obedience

Sin is devastating; it makes us ashamed – of our actions and ashamed of our thoughts that have led to our actions. Do I sin because I don't trust God? Usually – it's just plain disobedience, stubbornness, and not submitting to the Lord. I don't want to be found out of God's will. God knows I, along with many people, have struggled with the habit (addiction?) of gambling (mostly poker and slots) and pornography for so many years, off and on. Today, my son's 31st birthday, I submit and put it all at God's feet. I can do all things through Christ who strengthens me. I denounce these sins. God has already told me that when I continue to gamble and continue to watch pornography, spiritual and physical death is right at my doorstep. Sin when it has conceived gives birth to death. God spared my life so many years ago, in fact, just before he called me to the ministry. I make no more excuses for not obeying God.

We usually enjoy sin which lasts for a short while. However, just like drug binges, alcohol binges, food binges, or anything else in which we indulge that is damaging to our soul and relationship with God, we are left with regret and remorse the next day. Temperance is one of the gifts of the Spirit mentioned in Galatians, Chapter 5. Anything we do to excess, anything we put our trust in besides God, anything that feeds the earthly desires instead of our spiritual needs, leaves us open to satanic attack. It leaves us open to the enemies' jeers and degradation instead of God's cheers and salvation. We listen to the enemy and the evil desires of our hearts and give in to these soul-killers. Our hearts are deceitfully wicked. Paul says that the thing he wants to do, he does not, and the thing he does not want to do, that he does. He then asks, "Who will deliver me from this body of death?" (Romans 7:18-24)

God will. The Bible says that we have not resisted unto blood, striving against sin in our lives. (Hebrews 12:4) We talk about taking up our cross and carrying it the way Jesus did. This is easy to say and not so easy to do, all by ourselves. The enemy would make us believe we are all alone and that when we do fall (sin) that God has forsaken us. But the word says God will never leave us nor forsake us. (Hebrews 13:5) The word says that if we confess our sins he is faithful and just to forgive us our sins and cleanse us from all unrighteousness. (1 John 1:9) David broke every one of the 10 Commandments of the law of God. Among them were adultery, false witness, and murder. There is no little or big sin – it is all sin. David cried out to God for forgiveness and threw himself upon God's mercy. However, this was only after another human being (Samuel), who knew about David's sin, expertly and with stern conviction out of love for David, called it to David's attention. (2 Samuel 12:4-14)

This means our lives should be transparent, no matter how embarrassing we believe it to be. I disclose my sins because the Bible tells us to do so, and it keeps us accountable for being obedient to God. Even though God is omnipotent, omniscient, and omnipresent, sometimes we fool ourselves into thinking that God will not notice our dirty little secrets if we turn off the lights or hide in our closets. We think because no other human being (or no one we know) is aware at the moment of our secret sin, we're getting away with it. However, not only does God see and know all, our own conscience that is within every believer works in conjunction with the Holy Spirit. (Romans 9:1) It works to convict us. An unrepentant believer is a tortured soul. (Psalm 38:3) We lose fellowship and communion with God, as did Adam and Eve. (Genesis 3:22-24) We are banished from the loving and holy presence of Yahweh, who cannot and will not look upon sin. He is a loving God but he is also a God of judgment. He tells us that obedience is better than sacrifice. (1 Samuel 15:22) He talks to us constantly through his prophets: Isaiah, Ezekiel, Jeremiah, and Amos to name a few. "Trust and obey God!" "Deliver your souls from death!" "Turn away from sin and turn to the Holy One of Israel" are thundered in the streets and on the rooftops. Jesus, God's son (Yahoshua) repeatedly called the Pharisees and Sadducees a "generation of vipers." (Matthew 3:7; Matthew 12:34; Matthew 23:33) Jesus and the prophets all speak for God who is a loving father who only wants the best for his children.

It's a matter of obedience. It's not about our church attendance; it's not about our tithing; it's not about our preaching and teaching; it's not about the many gifts and talents we possess. Yes, all of these are part of service to God, but his main concern is our obedience to him and to his word. All disobedience is sin. God will speak to our hearts and specifically instruct us not to do something or to take some specific action. We then test the limits, as hard-headed children do, to see just how far to the edge of the cliff we can go before falling off. What loopholes can we find in the Word of God? What gray areas can we enlarge to help us by-pass God's instructions? What can we find or do so that our will be done?

God knows our earthly nature. He knows our hearts are "deceitful above all things, and desperately wicked." (Jeremiah 17:9) He makes provision for us. We must keep in constant communion with him. We are to turn to him, submit ourselves to him, and resist the enemy, who will flee. Jesus (Yahoshua) says he is the vine and we are the branches. We must stay connected to him if we are to survive spiritually. He tells us he is the living water of whom we must drink (John 4:10); he is the pearl of great price we must seek (Matthew 13:46); he is the way, the truth, and the life, and that no one comes to the Father except by him (John 14:6). He tells us to be obedient, the same thing our Father in Heaven tells us. Every man, woman, and child who is a believer is married to Christ. He is our husband, our bridegroom. (Matthew 25:1-13) Our marriage vows include obedience. We will never be ashamed if we obey him. We will never be discarded. We will become his trusted, tested, and tried angle-stones: stones of obedience that can be trusted to be used for his service – stones of obedience that are precious in his sight. (1 Peter 2:5)

God forgive me for all of my sins, especially my secret sins that I think no one knows about. Help me to be obedient to every word that proceeds out of your mouth. Help me to listen, trust, and obey your commands in your word. Take away everything within me that is not like you. Make me brand new. Help me to confess my sins before men, knowing that it is ultimately to you that I must give an account. Give me the courage to be transparent before men to keep accountable. May you have mercy on my soul and deliver me. Amen

A Test of Forgiveness

"And let us not be put to the test, but keep us safe from the Evil One. For if you let men have forgiveness for their sins, you will have forgiveness from your Father in heaven. But if you do not let men have forgiveness for their sins, you will not have forgiveness from your Father for your sins."
Matthew 6:13-15

Can you forgive anyone of anything? If so, how long does it take? What does it really mean to forgive? What does our relationship with the forgiven one look like afterwards? So many scriptures tell us to overlook wrongs (Prov. 19:11), to forgo revenge and wait for the Lord to handle the matter (Prov. 20:22), to turn the other cheek and go the extra mile when we are wronged and to love and do good to those who persecute us (Matthew 5:7, 29-47). The Bible even tells us to pray for them and ask God to bless them (Romans 12:14, 17, 19-21) and to quickly get rid of any anger, harsh words, or maliciousness we may have toward the wrongdoer (Ephesians 4:31-32).

I've heard followers of the Honorable Elijah Muhammad say that this kind of thinking was the slave master's way of making sure that the slaves suffered comfortably while they were being persecuted, that is, a way to make sure the slaves didn't rebel against their captors. In some ways this is true; however, Jesus (Yahoshua) himself instructed us to do these things. However, he also tells us to be harmless as doves and wise as serpents. (Matthew 10:16) He tells us to foresee the danger and go far from it. (Proverbs 22:3; Proverbs 27:12) If we are in a position to get away from the danger, I believe God wants us to flee from it. Whether or not we are able to flee from the danger, God wants us to forgive those who persecute or wrong us. Jesus (Yahoshua) did this on Calvary with his dying breath. (Luke 23:34)

Forgiveness is for the one doing the forgiving and also for the one who is forgiven. Un-forgivingness is like excess baggage that weighs heavily on a person. It stunts your spiritual growth, causes physical illness, and can lead to an early temporal death.

When you forgive, it removes a weight and burden from your shoulders. It lifts the scales from your eyes and heart and opens your ears up to listen to God's loving instructions. It moves you forward so you can press toward the mark of the prize of the high calling in Christ Jesus. It has a profound impact upon the forgiven one, if allowed to do so. The person catches a glimpse of God's forgiveness and we may witness the miracle of God's goodness that leads one to repentance. (Romans 2:4) This forgiven one, your former enemy, once converted, may be the very tool God wants to use for his service. That person may be on fire for God because "he who loves much he who is forgiven much." (Luke 7:47)

My forgiveness was put to the test when the man, who I lived with and loved before I was converted, physically molested my children. It is one thing to suspect such a thing; it is quite another to be presented with evidence by trained professional doctors from Martin Luther King Hospital (Los Angeles) who examined my children. Of course, this was only after a person in whom I confided my suspicions had called the police. I was forced to leave my two- and four-year old in the back of the police car after my little ones had just asked me if we were going to McDonald's. My heart and life was broken, blown to bits. I was charged with neglect – me, not my husband who never paid child support and helped me with my children – me! My children were in foster homes and then lived with my parents. We all had to go to counseling. I was subjected to so much pain, anguish, and degradation. I was persecuted and prosecuted. It would take six months and many life changes before I would be finally reunited with my children.

How can you forgive someone who has harmed your two little ones for whom you have and would give your own life? A mother will take a bullet for her children; a mother who does not know how to swim will jump into a lake to save her child who is drowning; a mother will do whatever it takes to protect her children. He was never convicted because the courts said the children were too young and confused to be good witnesses.

How do you forgive someone whose actions have caused the courts to say that you did not care enough about your children to protect them when you know this is not true? Our earthly minds and hearts want revenge and retribution. We want the person to pay for what he or she has done, not just legally, but with their own lives.

I never saw the perpetrator again; he never confessed and he never asked for my forgiveness. However, I had to forgive him for my sake. Before this, I remember having a dream where I saw him and approached him. He had a sinister smirk on his face. Suddenly, I realized I was holding a hatchet. Almost instinctually I grabbed it with both hands and swung it straight across his neck, cutting off his head. However, to my amazement, his head plopped right back down onto his neck. He stood there laughing at me. Immediately, I awoke. God spoke to me and made me realize that I was trying to kill a spirit. You may be able to kill the body of the evil person, but that spirit will remain. Only God can and will destroy these evil spirits when it is time. God reminded me that we war not against flesh and blood, but against principalities, and powers, and spiritual wickedness in high places. (Ephesians 6:12) My brother and cousins had told me that I needed only to give the word and the perpetrator would be "taken care of." As a woman of God, I knew this was not an option. I must answer to the Holy One of Israel. I could never intentionally take the life of another person, nor be an accomplice to such. I knew that I must obey God is all respects.

So, in my heart, I forgave the man who hurt my children and me. God took him out of my realm and I have never seen him again, although I will never forget his face. I've learned a hard lesson through this experience. I even remembered all of the things for which God forgave me and for which he continues to forgive me. The Bible tells us that if we do not forgive men, God will not forgive us. (Matthew 6:15) I forgave him as God tells us to do. I prayed for him and even asked God to bless him. It was not easy; it was one of the hardest things I've ever had to do in my life, but the battle is not ours, it's the Lord's. (Psalm 91:4)

> *God help me to forgive those who wrong me, even when they don't ask for forgiveness. Let the light of your word shine so brightly in my life that the wrongdoer will be led to repentance and ask, "What shall I do that I might be saved?   Amen*

Forgive Us Our Debts

A faithful man shall abound with blessings: but he that maketh haste to be rich shall not be innocent. He that hasteth to be rich hath an evil eye, and considereth not that poverty shall come upon him."
Proverbs 18:20, 22

When the disciples asked Jesus to teach them how to pray, he did so, and included toward the end, "and forgive us our debts as we forgive our debtors." (Matthew 6:12). Some of the translations say "transgressions" or "sins" instead of debts. I like to use the word "debts" because my constant prayer is that God will forgive my debts. I know he will; I just wish my creditors would.

I've been working since the age of nine. I've held so many jobs throughout my life, always supported myself and my family, and always made sure my children had a roof over their heads and never went without the essential life needs. I even supported my ex-husband before we were divorced. I never wanted to be rich or wealthy, although I always thought I would be. I remember when I was 16 years old. God was dealing with me even then. He impressed upon my mind two things I would experience or come to realize in my life: that death was a reality that we all have to face one day, and that I would be wealthy. I kept wondering ever since that time if the latter was a consolation because of the first. So, I grew up thinking I was going to be wealthy. I had a great mind, went to college, worked hard. Then life happened. To make a long story short: I filed bankruptcy three times; the first time (Chapter 7) in 1976 when my ex-husband and I ran up my credit cards and destroyed my credit; the second time (Chapter 7) in 1990, I filed but never completed it but the courts said it would still have to stay on my record for 10 years; and the third time in 2000 (Chapter 13). If things don't turn around, I may be facing this same situation in 2010. You can only file every 10 years.

Bankruptcy is not pretty. It's not something we want in our lives. The worst part of this is that the student loans and repayment for taxes the IRS says I owe usually are never forgiven during this process. These are "guaranteed" monies and must be repaid. I owe, altogether, approximately $140,000 – of which $10,000 in back taxes. My student loans come due and payable again this December. I believe they will no longer allow me the hardship forbearance. Interests alone, add an additional $20,000 each year. It appears I'll never get out of debt, unless something miraculous happens. I remember having a dream vision many years ago. I saw a little girl in the distance; she was sitting on top of a mountain. As I got a bit closer, I could see that the girl was crying. As I drew closer, I could see that the little girl was me! Finally, I noticed that the mountain on top of which I was sitting was made of cash, diamonds, gold, and other types of jewels that were all packed together so tightly that they formed the mountain on top of which I sat. Before I could open my mouth to form a question, God impressed his word on my mind and said, "You're sitting on your gifts."

It's true – God has given me many gifts, talents, and abilities. I had been using some of them but not to the capacity that God had intended. I've had people come up to me and tell me that God said that I would be a millionaire. Being wealthy means only one thing to me: that I would be able to pay my debts, contribute to God's work, build up the ministry, create jobs for others, and supply affordable housing and food for those in this country and other countries. I would be able to start schools and build care centers. I would be able to minister through other media to preach and teach the gospel. So far, the wealth has not materialized. I finally came to realize that I have contributed to my own poverty and hindered the blessings God has in store.

The Bible says that "eye has not seen, ear has not heard, nor entered into the heart of man what God has prepared for those who love him." (I Corinthians 2:9) The Bible also tells us that if we are faithful with a little we will be blessed with much.

(Matthew 25:21, 23) I know that I have not been a faithful steward. I have given tithes and offerings faithfully; however, a good part of the 90% has been used for gambling. The usual bills were paid; however, playing poker and especially slot machines is an expensive form of recreation. You're sucked in with the notion that you're going to hit it big. After all, haven't you seen others win big bucks? I was sucked into this in 1989 when I discovered Fort McDowell, just 9 miles away from where I was living in Scottsdale when I worked for Motorola. Then Casino Arizona arrived that was virtually down the street from where I lived. During that time, you heard and/or saw people winning a million dollars almost every week. The person was spotlighted in the casino and in the newspaper. Then everything changed. The "drug" dealers now had you hooked. They re-programmed the computers and went to printing winning tickets instead of having the slot patrol cash out coins. There have been progressively less and less winners. It's a big deal today when someone wins $50,000 or $100,000. People have watched ordinary people like Chris Moneymaker win the World Series of Poker through a satellite ticket he won. He didn't even have to pay the $10,000 buy-in and he won over a $1,000,000! He did this online.

Looks lucrative, doesn't it? However, we have been duped into thinking we can get rich quick. The Bible tells us to work to get what we need. Even in economic times such as these, we need only trust God. David, a man after God's own heart, said, "I am young and now old but never have I seen the righteous forsaken nor his seed begging bread." (Psalm 37:25) God will supply our every need. We may not have lots of riches and wealth but he will supply everything we need. Palm 34:10 says, "The young lions do lack and suffer hunger but they that seek the Lord shall not want any good thing." Jesus confirms this. He tells us that if we abide in him and his words abide in us, we can ask what we want and he will do it. (John 15:7) Gambling or anything built on getting rich quick will surely lead to our poverty while lining the pockets of casino owners and those who present us with these get rich quick schemes. Hard work, diligence, "casting our bread upon many waters," obedience to

God's commands, and being a faithful steward will ensure that we are delighting ourselves in the Lord as stated in Psalm **34:4** and he will give us the desires of our hearts.

> *God, I confess that I have not been a good and faithful steward with all that you have blessed me. Please forgive me and help me to pay my debts, to abstain from activities that are unprofitable, and to become diligent and patient. I know that you will bless me with all that I need. Help me to stand on the promises of your word. Amen*

The Right to Choose Life

"And the Lord God made man from the dust of the earth,
breathing into him the breath of life:
and man became a living soul." Genesis 2:7

There has been and continues to be so much controversy over abortion: its legality, its immorality, whether it's a choice or even whether one has the right to make this choice. If so, who has this choice? Some Christians are so fanatical when it comes to this issue – that is, they protest with signs and marches in front of abortion clinics. They value the life of an unborn child so much that they even resort to planting bombs that explode and destroy the clinics, along with everyone inside. They are convinced that God condones their actions. There are others who are so fanatical about their right to make this choice that they convince themselves, even against all presented scientific evidence, that the unborn is really not a human being at all. They convince themselves that the unborn is only a glob of blood and cells, so they're not really taking the life of a person. Along with this argument, they also convince themselves that since the "tissue" is inside the body of the pregnant person it is that person's right to decide what to do and what not to do. So, who's right?

I remember the day I discovered that I was a murderer – I believe the legal phrase would be an accessory to murder. The person who directly committed the murder was actually a hired killer – by me. Over a span of 17 years I had committed this same crime a total of four times. I've had four abortions in my life. The doctors were the hired killers. I paid them to take the life of my unborn children. The first time was when I was 18 years old. I was not close to God at that time, my live-in boyfriend who would later become my husband, was financially unable to take care of me, let alone a family. I would end up aborting another of his children. When I aborted a child I convinced myself that it was out of survival. However, it would have been better to take precautions beforehand or abstain altogether. It's not easy when you're finally being noticed as a

23

woman after suffering with an inferiority complex most of your life. Now you have contacts and have fixed your broken tooth. Little did I realize I was spiritually blind and my life was now broken.

The other two abortions were not my ex-husbands. One was a white man who I learned later used drugs and was just plain irresponsible. However, I had given my life to the Lord even though I had fallen back into sin. I knew abortion was wrong in God's eyes and I was going to have the child. However, I made the mistake of confiding in the black male attorney who worked for The Dial Corporation where I was employed at the time. Although he professed to be a Christian, he manipulated me, for whatever reason – maybe he thought I would be an embarrassment to him at the company – maybe he thought he was doing it for my own good. He made he think that if I had the abortion there would be a possibility of he and I getting together later on. Mind you, he had also conveniently stated that he never became involved with someone with whom he worked. Of course, the week I announced that I had taken another job, he also announced that he was engaged to someone else. The last abortion was the "love-child" of a black man with whom I worked at Motorola and I later discovered was what he called a "white witch." Nonetheless, I had determined I would have the child. However, he had been living with another woman and was going to marry her. He threatened to run me down with a vehicle if I didn't have the abortion. I acquiesced. This time, he paid the killer.

I finally changed my lifestyle and submitted myself back to Christ. I had two children before the last two abortions, both by my ex-husband. I finally started trusting God. It would be many, many years and many, many tears later before I could finally forgive myself for what I had done. I admire the women I've met who have 8, 10 or more children. Yes, they may struggle, but I have seen God bless them. I know women with this number of children who have at least one professional athlete in the family. Guess what? They do not have to worry about financial security – one of the very reasons I aborted my children. It is God who created life and it is only he who is allowed to take it away. God commands us not to murder. (Exodus 20:13) Abortion is murder, plain and simple. War is murder, plain and simple. We take away innocent lives without their consent. They are the only ones who should be allowed to make the choice to choose life. It is an inherent right that God put within each of us – those whose voices you can hear and those whose voices you cannot.

Jesus said that he came that we might have life and that more abundantly. (John 10:10) He told Nicodemus that if he wanted to see the Kingdom of Heaven he must be born again. (John 3:7) Before a person can be born again, he or she must first be allowed to be born. God breathed his spirit into us. He gave us a free will. We are free to make choices when it is within our power to do so. However, each of us must suffer the consequences for our choices. God makes sure that we have all of the information (Bible) beforehand so that we can make intelligent and right choices. It is only by the grace of God that I am still alive. My uterine lining could have torn and I could have bled to death, as many women have. A natural health doctor, an iridologist (eye specialist), looked into my eyes and guessed that I had previously had an abortion. He told me that having an abortion can be likened to a person travelling in a car down the road at 80 miles per hour and then suddenly, without warning, throwing the car into Reverse. He said if you can imagine what this does to a car, just think what it does to your body. I believe the abortions are part of the reasons I was pre-med in college. I was going to become an OB-GYN. However, God made me a healer of hearts instead. I serve as a mid-wife for God and now give birth to and assist in the birth of ministries.

God, it is only by your grace that I have not been destroyed in my ignorance. Please forgive me for throwing away that which you have created. I want to always put my trust in you and in nothing else. I know that life is so precious in your sight – both physical and especially spiritual life. Let me exercise your free will to make not just the right choice but the righteous choice. Amen

Death Be Not Proud

"O' death, where is thy sting? O' grave, where is thy victory?"
I Corinthians 15:55

Death – the cessation of life – it comes to every living thing. It is the final part of the cycle of life. However, God put within every living creature the instinct of survival. This instinct has nothing to do with intelligence, reasoning, or logic. For example, it is physically impossible for anyone to hold his or her breath until he or she dies. Even people who commit suicide only succeed when they create conditions that defy all physical laws. For example, a person who leaps from a 10-story building is defying the Law of Gravity. A person who jumps into the river is defying the law of the body's respiration system and the laws of motion. Also, these people are defying God's Law against Murder, even self-murder. When we give our lives to Christ, our lives no longer belong to us; our lives belong to God. Therefore, suicide is also defying God's Law against Stealing: taking something that does not belong to us.

The Bible says that it is "appointed unto man once to die, but after this the judgment" (Hebrews 9:27). You mean we are judged after we die? How can that be? This means there is a second death. I remember how I was so afraid of dying – so much so that I used to have anxiety attacks. The last time was in 1987 when I was riding the bus in Los Angles. I had been having such episodes periodically and they were coming more frequently. I couldn't explain it; I felt a sense of complete and utter darkness and nothingness, as though I was in a lonely, dark, and silent pit and there was nothing there, not even me. I did not know it at the time, but God was giving me a glimpse of what the second death is like. Christ experienced this impending second death when he prayed incessantly that the cup of death he was to drink would pass from him. Finally, Christ experienced the actual second death on the cross. It is dark nothingness and the separation from God. We are made in the likeness of God. He breathed into us his spirit and we became living souls. (Genesis 1:26-27) When God removes his spirit, that soul – that self – that part of you ceases to be. Unless Jesus raises one from the dead, the dead do not speak; they do not come back to haunt you; they do not come back to help you; and they do not wander the streets looking for rest.

The enemy made me believe that, if I gave my heart and life to Christ, I was going to die. The enemy is a liar and the father of lies. He is also a deceiver. He gives half-truths. A great and delicious-looking meal laced with poison is deadly nonetheless. Yes, I was going to die. I was going to die to self and sin. Eventually, unless the Lord returns beforehand, I will die physically. I had just come home from watching porno movies. My live-in boyfriend was at work. I had been trying to get a divorce from my husband who had been gone for four years. My two children were at school. I remember that I put my key up to the back door knob, mind you I didn't touch the knob; I just put it up to the knob. I felt something snatch the keys to the ground! I stepped back. It took me by surprise; I couldn't believe what just happened. Cautiously, I picked up the keys. This caused me to focus on the key ring that I'd bought a while back but never thought much of until that day. It said: "Please be patient with me, God isn't finished with me yet." Right then I heard God speak to my spirit: "I will be finished with you if you keep this up." My heart started racing. The next few days I had out-of-body experiences. I would be up on the ceiling and couldn't see what was under me, nor could I come down. I would be under the bed. I would be flying around the city. One time, I thought I was awake and had gotten up to open the door, but my hand went through the knob. I would learn later that my spirit was eventually leaving my body. God was allowing me to experience the spiritual realm – that realm I had been so afraid of – that realm that had been haunting me.

One night after this, I would learn that it was time to face reality: I was soon to die. It was late at night and everyone was asleep. I couldn't sleep. I was standing just above the floor heater in the hallway facing the front door. To my right was the living room and to my left was our bedroom. I was at a cross-road in my life. I had to make a choice. I didn't realize just how significant my situation was: standing on the heater represented how urgent my situation had become – I was burning up in my own sin; the living room to my right was just that – a choice for life; the bedroom to my left was the choice of sin. Because I was not married, my bed had become defiled. In a twinkling of a moment, I saw Christ with his arms outstretched to me as if to say, "Come to me." There were never any words from either of us. I started to cry. I wanted to come to him but I was too weak. I loved my boyfriend more than I loved Christ because I did not know Christ. I had been baptized at the age of nine but never knew the love of Christ, never really read and studied the word of God. In my heart, I kept pleading with Christ to help me because I couldn't help myself.

I chose to go back into the bedroom. When I lay down on the bed, immediately I couldn't breathe. I didn't know what it was but it caused me to cough and cough. No one in the house awoke then or throughout any of the experiences I had. I got up from the bed and went into the living room. As soon as I lay down on the couch, the coughing stopped; however, I could no longer feel my body. There was this loud ringing and light so bright I could not look into it. It's hard to describe in words, but there were two lights: one was greater than the other. I knew I was in the presence of God. The Holy Spirit had taken me up into the Third Heaven. There was a conversation going on about me. No words were spoken, yet I knew. God was going to take my life that night. Christ was making intercession for me. He said, "Father, give her time, I know she'll come to me." At that moment, I heard my children crying for me. I felt an urgency to get back to them. Suddenly, I was aware of my body. I thought I'd been asleep but I hadn't. Immediately, I ran into my children's room to see about them. They were fast asleep. Everyone was asleep.

It was after this that I allowed God to perform spiritual surgery on me. I gave my life to prayer, reading and studying the

Bible, went to church, and submitted my life to Christ. I received my call to the ministry and changed my lifestyle. I gave up the man I loved for the man who loved me. God told me he wanted me to come home. This meant back to Arizona where I was born and back to the loving Father and expert fisher of men. I became dead to sin and alive to righteousness. I know that when I fall, and I do fall, that the man who loves me, who is my husband now, is right there to help me, to pick me up, to catch me, and is forever making intercession for me. O' death, where is thy sting; O' grave, where is thy victory? (I Corinthians 15:55)

God, thank you for sending your Son to die on the cross for me. Thank you for never giving up on me. Thank you, Jesus, my Savior, for making intercession for me. Let this experience serve as the gauge in my commitment to you; let it serve as the faithful reminder to deflect the enemy's darts of doubt. Let my life be submitted to you that I will always choose your "living room of righteousness" instead of my "dying room of sin." Amen

Can We Handle The Truth?

"And you shall know the truth, and the truth shall make you free."
John 8:32

As Christians we feel we are to be color blind, that is, race, ethnicity, natural origin, and the color of one's skin should not matter. We are all the same in God's eyes – or are we? It is not man who made differences, whether those differences are color of skin, eyes, facial features, hair texture, size and frame, quality of voice, aptitude, ability, temperament, intelligence, and values. We are each wired differently. God made different species, different types of flowers in his garden – differences abound in this world in which we live. It is one thing to appreciate the differences in others and in things in life; it is quite another to esteem, especially when it comes to people, one race over another, a skin color over another, hair texture over another, and facial features over another. We are not color blind; no one is. We see the differences. We should love ourselves, who we are, and what we look like. We were made in the image of God. When I say "we" I mean those who know who they are in God, the one true God, Yah. These are the Black Hebrew Israelites.

The truth is not easy to accept and sometimes it's not so easy to voice. It takes courage on the part of both the communicator and the receiver. The enemy is a liar from the beginning. Everything that God created, the Devil created a counterfeit. God formed man from the dust of the ground, that is, from dirt, which is black and brown. The original Scriptures tell the truth of the likeness of the first man and woman. History books and research tells the truth: we know that the true Hebrew was not a Jew; this is something they created and crafted to cover up the truth. Our Lord and Savior was not a man of European descent; he was a man of African descent, as were the Hebrews. His name was not Jesus, which is the name variation of a pagan God; his name was and is Yahoshua. There was never and is not a letter "J" in the Hebrew Language.

Hollywood has performed its magic and for hundreds and hundreds of years has made people believe a lie. If those of European descent knew their true history, I believe they would be unable to handle it. There are three videos worth watching: *Hebrew or the So-Called Negro, Children of the Fallen Ones, and Your Fathers Have Taught You Lies* (www.cofah.com).

Despite the hundreds and hundreds of years of oppression, the lies, the degradation, the rape, the murder, the lynching, and the awful deprivation of heritage, home, and heart, God commands us to love. Aside from being patient and kind, not behaving unseemly, not seeking its own, and not vaunting up itself, love keeps no record of wrongs that have been committed. As Black Hebrew Israelites, we are called to take to "all the world" the gospel of salvation, the light of Yah's word, the truth that sets one free. We are to be witnesses within our immediate homes and borders and then to the "uttermost parts of the earth." For years Black Hebrew Israelites were made to believe we are the Gentiles that the Bible talks about. This is what we were taught and made to believe. This was part of the cover-up. TV and the movie industry reinforced it. It continues until this very day. We are the light that shines in a dark place. We are the beacons that expose the hidden things and light the way to true salvation. The apostle Paul said that he is not a Hebrew who is one outwardly, but inwardly. True circumcision is of the heart not just of the flesh. (Romans 2:29) When we allow the light of Yahoshua's sacrifice and love to penetrate us and change us, we reflect the true image of Yah. This image has nothing to do with the color of our skin or our heritage. We are fallen mankind who needed the Savior to reconcile us back to God. Our Father, who cannot look upon sin, sees repentant mankind washed in the Blood of the Lamb. Our lives become "white as snow," that is purified. Skin color has nothing to do with purification or lack thereof. This only has to do with melanin or lack thereof. Is God color blind? Of course he isn't. He sees us as we are: in our sins – tainted with stains unto death; once born again, he sees us in the sanctified, pure, and living image of His Son Jesus (Yahoshua).

God, Father Yah, I have been living a lie most of my life. Help me to accept the truth of your word and to dispel the darkness within my own heart. Let me love the way you loved. Let me forgive those who hated me without a cause. Help those who I or my ancestors may have oppressed to forgive me and them. Recreate in me a clean heart and renew a right spirit within me. Wash me in your blood on a daily basis." Amen

Are We There Yet?

"I waited patiently for the Lord; and he inclined unto me, and heard my cry."
Psalm 40:1

There is an old saying, "God is never late; he may not come when you want him to, but he's always right on time." Many of us, who have ever waited for anything or asked God for something and had to wait, know this to be true. However, the wait is not always easy. One can be 30 years old and seek an answer from God. God will say, "Wait a minute," and before you know it, you're now 60 years old. God made time for man; however, God is not bound by such laws. He will usually answer, as most loving fathers do, with either a "Yes," "No," or sometimes there is silence. I believe the silence is the hardest of all. This is when faith and patience come into play.

We live in the fast-paced microwave generation. Though technology has had a positive effect on the way we conduct business, it has also created a mind-set where time is a commodity equated with money. Time, as is money, is a valuable resource, nothing more, nothing less. It is no longer utilized in the way God intended. People spend the first half of their lives, that is, valuable time that cannot be regained and losing their health in the process, trying to get wealthy. They use the wealth they have created to find ways to save more time to make more money. What a cycle. Then, when time has worn down their finite, mortal, and temporal lives, they spend the last part of their lives trying to get healthy again. Time waits for no man.

I used to be one of the most impatient people there were. I drove fast, walked fast, and talked fast. It always seemed to me that people intentionally got in their cars, turned in front of me, and insisted on driving below, what I called at the time, the "suggested" speed limit. I was never one to use much foul language or give people the finger. However, I found my horn to be the best invention since the green light. When people would turn in front of me or drive slower than I wanted to go, I would lay on the horn with such intensity that I might as well have given them the finger or cursed them out. As people of God, our consciences work with the Holy Spirit to convict us, especially when reading the Bible. It always has the effect of changing us from glory to glory. Along with this God chastens us. I was about to lose my toy.

One day, I made the mistake of asking God to give me more patience. Of course, I didn't do as the old saying, "God give me patience and do it now!" But God is not slack concerning his promises. He knows what you have a need for even before you ask. I found myself in one of my similar predicaments. A person turned in front of me. Of course I laid on my faithful horn of salvation. There was no sound. I did it again. Still no sound. I was so frustrated. All I could say was, "Get 'em, Lord!" God had taken away my sounding board. Not only did I learn patience for other drivers, but I learned to slow down in life. It became more of a reality from the stories I heard after September 11, 2001, the day the world mourned. A pastor told of how he had missed that fatal flight. Another person told how they were stuck in traffic and couldn't make it to work to the Trade Center that day. It does us well to wait patiently on God and not insist on our own way. We cannot see around the corners or in the darkness of the alley. Also, we should never be weary in well doing. This is also part of patience. Patience is long-suffering. It builds character. It builds stamina. It is a wonderful fruit of righteousness and one of the gifts of the Spirit. (Galatians 5:22-23) Once developed in us, we become trees of righteousness whereby others can find rest and shade and possibly partake of our fruit and utilize the seeds to sow beautiful patient spirits within themselves and in others.

> *God, forgive me for trusting in everything except for you. Help me not to weary in well doing. Help me to wait patiently on you. Help me to seek your face before taking action. Help me to wait faithfully for your answer no matter how long it may take. Help me to use your resource of time in the way you intend. Let me not waste it, not even one precious minute."* *Amen*

Not Without My Armor

"Finally, my brethren, be strong in the Lord, and in the power of his might. Put on the whole armour of God, that ye may be able to stand against the wiles of the devil. For we wrestle not against flesh and blood, but against principalities, against powers, against the rulers of the darkness of this world, against spiritual wickedness in high places." Ephesians 6:10-12

No one wakes up one day and decides to become a pedophile, a rapist, a homosexual, an adulterer, or a fornicator – nor is this type of behavior instinctual. Despite what philosophers or well-meaning scientists or modern moralists will tell you, the foregoing type of behaviors are learned habits. They are the symptoms of and the direct result of a sinful heart. The Bible says that out of the abundance of the heart the mouth speaks, but also out of the abundance of the heart the hands act. It is well known that children love candy, but not all children. Children who love candy have been conditioned to do so by their parents, older siblings, friends, neighbors, even teachers and friendly neighborhood doctors. However, there are children who have never had candy because their parents did not believe it was healthy and so never spoiled them with this kind of treat. These children don't see it as a treat because they haven't been conditioned to view it as such.

The act of sex, of making love, was created in man by God, but it was created for two consenting married adults: one male and one female. Anything outside of this is what God calls sin, an aberration, an unnatural act, an abomination against God. However, society has its own particular set of morals or lack thereof. Certain acts are viewed as acceptable while others are noted as "reprehensible" and worthy of arrest, conviction, and incarceration – that is, provided the perpetrator is caught and brought to justice.

Most sexual sins committed against a child or a person will eventually be reciprocated if gone unchecked and unseen, especially if endured over a long period of time. It does not excuse the behavior from either party but it does explain it. Sex is so powerful that it creates life when a man and woman engage in it at the right moment in time. God created us as sexual beings and made a way for it to be enjoyed in the right context. The enemy's goal has always been to exploit, manipulate, and pervert what God has created with the goal to destroy. God creates, man procreates, and the enemy entices man with his evil devices to kill, steal, and destroy. (John 10:10)

TV and the movie industry have contributed greatly to the romanticizing of sexual sins. A great number of producers, movie executives, advertising executives, and company CEO's are astute and calculating. At one point in time, the visual media reflected real life or situations that appeared to be like real life. The goal was to create movies, shows, and commercials targeted to specific groups to sell specific products. Eventually, the media became so powerful, they have used it to control how the masses think; they tell us what is morally acceptable, they tell us what is fashionable to wear, they tell us what it best to consume – in so doing, they mold our behavior to fit their agenda. It is a multi-billion dollar a year business. It is the lust of the flesh, the lust of the eyes, and the lust of the world. It is everything Jesus (Yahoshua) warned us against.

It is true we, who are believers, are not of this world, but we do live in this world. (John 17:14) As such, we need protection from these advertised and learned society-accepted "treats." God has already made provision for us. It is easy to become a victim of and a perpetrator of sexual sins when you are naked. God has given us the best covering and has told us to put it on daily: the whole armor of God. (Ephesians 6:10-18) These are our defensive and offensive weapons. With this armor, we are "dressed to kill." No wiles of the devil and his enticements can persuade us nor harm us. Our hearts, our minds, our souls are protected. Our faith is shielded. Our witness is sure. God's truth keeps the armor safely in place. The word of God tears down the fake and false morality of the world. It replaces our weakness with the mighty righteousness of Christ. A new behavior is learned. A new creature is born.

New habits are formed. The armor that once felt heavy and constricting is now light and uplifting. It has become a part of our every day wardrobe. No sexual sin or otherwise can penetrate the powerful armor. The mind and heart are renewed from day to day. The Holy Spirit polishes the armor until it shines so brightly that the darkness of sexual sin is dispelled at the first thought. So, each day when we begin to "pack" to travel through this sinful world, one thought reigns supreme within us: "Not without my armor; not today; not ever."

God, I have been guilty of some type of sexual sin in my life. Others have abused me also. I forgive them for these terrible acts as you forgive me. I know there is no little or big sin – that it is all abominable sin in your eyes and that it leads to death. I choose life. So, thank you for your powerful armor of protection. Let me never leave home without it. Amen

Beyond My Foolishness

"When I consider thy heavens, the work of thy fingers, the moon and the stars, which thou hast ordained; What is man, that thou art mindful of him? and the son of man, that thou visitest him? For thou hast made him a little lower than the angels, and hast crowned him with glory and honour."
Psalm 8:3-5

My mother used to say, "God takes care of fools and babies, and you're no baby anymore." I can pinpoint some of the times in my life when my guardian angel was at work; however, I'm most certain that thousands of times I have been unaware that I was being protected. Sometimes it's the deep sense of impending danger and the quiet urging; sometimes it's the touch as if coming from a physical hand; other times it's the still quiet voice that speaks to my spirit. When you've spent enough time communicating with God, you begin to recognize his voice.

When I was younger I used to think I was being paranoid; however, paranoia turned into truth. I was attending USC in Los Angeles and had walked to Kentucky Fried Chicken to have a snack before catching the bus to go home where I lived with my parents in Gardena. I was sitting at one end of the wooden table in the park area which was mid-way between the campus and the bus stop. A man in his mid-thirties sat down near me. He struck up a casual conversation. Out of the corner of my eye, I could see a younger man come and sit down at the other end of the table mid-way from where my purse and food were sitting on the table. Immediately, a sense of urgency came upon me to grab my purse, leave the food and just go straight to the bus. I did this without hesitation and without thinking about it. When I reached the bus stop, I turned around to look back. The two men were talking and leaving together. I realized that they had plotted and planned to steal my purse. God's angel was protecting me.

Another time, my brother needed to go to the Employment Office. It was extremely early in the morning. I was tired and sleepy. I don't remember now why I had to go with him. He had his own car and he was the one driving. I didn't even go inside with him; I stayed in the car. The windows were rolled up, and in spite of myself, I lied down on the front seat and fell asleep. I have no idea how long my brother was inside. It must have been at least an hour. I reluctantly awoke because someone kept nudging me. It was hard to wake up. At the time, I wasn't sure why. The hand kept nudging me and prompting me to roll down the window. Finally, I managed to roll down the window. It almost hurt to breathe. I opened the car door also. I turned around and no one was there. I realized that the hand of God had protected me. Had it not been for God, in my foolishness, I would have suffocated in that car and not be alive to write and tell about it.

I believe my guardian angel has had to work overtime. I remember many years later, I was living in Phoenix and attending the University of Phoenix. By this time, I had been married, divorced, and had two children – not necessarily all in that order. I worked full-time, went to school full-time, my children were both in diapers, and I didn't have a car. My classes were in the evening and I had to catch the bus. The walk home was not long but it was usually dark. I remember one night while walking home, something told me to not go the same way I usually go, to go around the other way. As I did this, I notice down the other side where I normally walked was a rustling in the bushes. I ran all the way home. I realized that someone had been watching me and knew my regular route. That person was waiting for me. Again, it was only by the grace of God. I found a way to get a ride to classes after that.

To think that God made man just a little lower than the angels – these created messengers of God, these beings who do God's bidding, these beings who continually cry "Holy, holy, holy" in the presence of almighty Yah. (Psalm 8:5; Hebrews 2:7, 9) Yet, when all is said and done, God says we will even judge the angels in Heaven. (I Corinthians 6:3) What humbleness of heart, mind, and spirit we should feel to realize that God loves us so much and cares about every aspect of our lives that he sends his messengers to watch over us. Tears stream down my corruptible and mortal cheeks "when I think of the goodness of God," as the songwriter exclaims, "and all he has done for me." Yes, "my soul cries out, Hallelujah. Thank God for saving me!"

> *God, I thank you for your ministering angels and for your divine protection. Let my ears, my eyes, and my steps continue in astute obedience to your prompting and to your will. Why you love me, Lord, I'll never know; but that you love me, I'll never forget. Amen*

Here I Am, Send Me

"Blessed are ye, when men shall revile you, and persecute you, and shall say all manner of evil against you falsely, for my sake. Rejoice, and be exceeding glad: for great is your reward in heaven: for so persecuted they the prophets which were before you." Matthew 5:11-12

Many seasoned and mature people of God have warned us, "Be careful what you pray for; you just might get it." I prayed for patience and got it with a sacrifice and hard lessons learned. I was so miserable with my ex-husband that I told God, "I don't want to be married." Of course, I meant that I did not want to be married to my ex-husband, but from our mouths to God's ears. I've been divorced for 26 years and it doesn't look I'll ever be married again. However, my one real regret when it came to petitioning God for something would be the time when my faith in serving God was so weak, that I decided to put God to the test. I said, "God, if you really want me to serve you, I need you talk to me the way you did Moses." I wanted to hear the Lord's voice, so that I would truly know this thing was real. Never mind that years prior during my conversion, God had delivered me from both physical and spiritual death. I wanted to hear his voice speaking to my spirit like he did with Moses. Who was I to ask such a thing? However, God spoke to me, but I was in no way prepared for what God was going to say, how he was going to use me, and more importantly, what he was going to give me to speak.

I know personally and firsthand the anguish, the sacrifice, the pain, and the humiliation that the prophets experienced. How many people are prepared to drink of this cup from the master's hand? At one time God told me he was sending me forth in the spirit of Jeremiah. God would give me a message to speak to the people and tell me that they will not listen to me. I questioned God as to why he would give me something to proclaim knowing that no one would listen to me. He said, "Because in that day, they can never say that they were not told." To be sent in this capacity is extremely difficult, but it is even more so when you are female, divorced, black, poor, and have no recognized title within the church. I was all of these. To obey God, I would have to use testimony time in the church to speak God's words. Like Moses, I did not really want to be used this way. I just wanted God to speak to *me*; I didn't want to speak *for* God. Sometimes God would use me to write a letter to the pastor; sometimes I would speak in tongues and interpret; sometimes I had to speak directly to one individual. I didn't like being God's instrument of warning and of discipline. But can the thing made say to the maker, "Why did you make me thus?" (Isaiah 29:16)

I spent a great deal of time in prayer. I had a prayer journal. I started it by putting down the names of every living person, organization, and group I had ever met and/or been a part of. I would pray daily and go down the list. Before long, I included prayers for those who needed it and would indicate the need to the right of the name. When the prayer was answered, I would note it. When someone on the list passed away, I would note it. Then, God would start to show me various things about specific individuals for which I was praying. He started to show me the end of their lives. If this was not painful enough, he began to command that I speak forth words, not to the person whose life was being taken, but to the congregation. The words God gave me were never to say that a person was going to die; God is so expert is how he does things. In fact, the person was never present. However, those who were in tuned with God knew from what I spoke what God was saying. I would be so torn and overwrought. I couldn't believe it. At first I thought surely this is not true, that I must be imagining it. I would ask God for confirmation, which he would give each time. I would receive confirmation through providence, through visions and dreams, through words spoken by others, through actions of others, and through the Scriptures God would give me.

I was mocked and ridiculed. I'm sure people thought I was unstable. I developed a Jonah-complex. However, people started to believe when those things started to come true. Still, I felt so destroyed. I knew God's hand and anointing was upon me, but it was hard to bear. The prophets suffered degradation, humiliation, were ostracized, were beaten (Joseph), hung upside down in a cistern (Jeremiah), commanded to eat cakes made with dung (Ezekiel), commanded to marry and bear children with a harlot (Hosea), sent to proclaim judgment to stiff-necked and disobedient people of God (Jonah), given visions and dreams of coming judgment (John), pronounce death upon individuals – to name just a few of their trials. Reluctant as many of them were, they eventually obeyed God. (Moses) They had been prepared for the office they would fulfill. However, they received on-the-job training. (Samuel) They received the tests first and the lessons later. They sacrificed many things, including love, marriage, and sometimes their lives. They humbled themselves before God to be used for his service. (Daniel) God highly exalted them for their obedience. The greatest prophet of all, our Messiah, paid the ultimate price for us. Nothing we go through in this life will ever compare to his obedience, trials, and sufferings before, during, and after Calvary.

God, you said in your word that life and death are in the power of the tongue. When you do speak to me, give me the obedience and the courage to speak only what you give me – not to add or detract from your message. I now know that it is a privilege to be used for your service and that my status and image is of no consequence for the sake of your Kingdom. May your spirit and your will lovingly guide me and that I represent you in all I say and do. Amen

From Here to Eternity

"For the preaching of the cross is to them that perish foolishness; but unto us which are saved it is the power of God." I Corinthians 1:18

Jesus said that there is no end to the making of books, and he was right. Hundreds of thousands of titles are published every year. However, one book outsells them all: the Bible. The Bible, originally penned in Greek, Hebrew, and Aramaic, has been translated in more languages than any other manuscript on the face of the earth. One must study to determine the cultural context, the historical context, the apocalyptic context, and to know when scripture should be taken literally or figuratively. The Bible can be read for devotion time to draw closer to God for peace and comfort, for literary study, for praise and worship, for poetic enjoyment, and for spiritual growth, to name a few of its purposes.

As a babe in Christ and to the word of God in 1987, I only knew of one reason to read the Bible: to gain knowledge of its contents. So, I, a legend in my own mind who was an avid reader, an astute college student, decided to read the entire Bible from cover to cover. After all, I thought, it's just like any other book. I felt that once I read it from beginning to end I would know everything there is to know about this "mysterious" book. After all, I had been reading since I was very young. I started off reading children's stories; then I graduated to *Mad* Magazines, then romance novels, then Agatha Christie mystery novels, biographies and autobiographies, and then all types of self-help books. Later I would become an English major and even Shakespeare would no longer evade my intellectual pursuit. However, I still believed a book written by "simple" men could not be so hard to understand.

I started at Genesis because, after all, one always starts at the beginning and then reads to the end. There are 66 books total: 39 in the Old Testament and 27 in the New Testament. I found myself reading the King James Version. I sat down in a comfortable chair and decided that I would read until I got tired, sleepy, or needed to attend to the children or some household chore. I found the stories enlightening, uplifting, intriguing, and interesting. However, I came to a standstill in the 22nd chapter of Genesis. God was putting Abraham to the test by asking Abraham to sacrifice his son Isaac. I have a son; I could not image God asking me to sacrifice my son, my only son, and my first born. Also, after all that Abraham and Sarah went through just to conceive Isaac, how could God do this? I put the book down and decided to read no further. It would not be until a month later that I decided to try it again. Maybe, I thought, I missed something. Again, I started from the beginning. Once again, everything was fine until I got to the 22nd chapter of Genesis. I couldn't take it. Isaac was the son of promise. Abraham and Sarah were well past child-bearing age, and God had already stated that Ishmael, Abraham's son by Hagar, was not the son through whom Abraham's seed would be like the stars in the sky and the sand in the sea. What kind of God is that?

I called my friend, Michael. Michael would tell me later that he didn't think I would become as strong in God as I would become because of my response to him when he witnessed to me about not going to hell. I had told him that I wasn't worried about going to hell because I would be so busy shaking hands with friends that I wouldn't have time to worry. I told Michael my problem and stumbling block. Michael, the good and patient little seed-planter that he was, told me that I was starting in the wrong place. I was beside myself. What do you mean I'm starting in the wrong place? I asked him. I told him I was starting at the beginning. No, he said, you're starting in the wrong place. He told me to go to the New Testament and start reading Matthew, Mark, Luke, John, and the rest of the New Testament. He said that I should then come back to the beginning and start reading the Old Testament. I thanked him and did as he suggested.

The most amazing thing happened! By the time I finished the New Testament, God had saved my soul. In conjunction with reading the Bible, I was introduced to a book called *The Desire of Ages* by Ellen White. I finally understood who Christ is. I developed a personal relationship with him. The word tells us that before we can get to God, we have to first come to Jesus (Yahoshua). (John 14:6) My understanding was beginning to open up. By the time I got to Genesis, the 22nd chapter, I could go on a little further. When Isaac asks his father where the lamb was for the burnt offering, Abraham says, "My son, God will provide himself a lamb for the burnt offering." (Genesis 22:8) I discovered that God was putting Abraham's obedience to the test, that God was not actually requiring Abraham to sacrifice his only son. However, God will never ask us to do anything he is not willing to do or hasn't done himself. God provided himself a lamb; his name is Jesus (Yahoshua), God's only begotten son. When I realized that Jesus (Yahoshua) was not only a great man and prophet, but he is God and that he loved me so much that he gave all that he had just for me. (John 3:16) I found the Bible to be my source for continual conversion and cleansing. My "great" intellect had finally taken its rightful place and come under subjection to the "foolishness" of the gospel.

> *Abba Father, words cannot express my gratitude for your sacrifice and your patience amid all of my foolishness. Help me to give myself to daily meditation and study of your Holy Word. Let it continue to be a lamp unto my feet and a light unto my path so that I may continue to grow thereby. Amen*

Joy Comes in the Morning

"My heart is sore pained within me: and the terrors of death are fallen upon me. Fearfulness and trembling are come upon me, and horror hath overwhelmed me. And I said, Oh that I had wings like a dove! For then would I fly away, and be at rest." Psalm 55:4-6

Suicide – self-murder. The church has debated over this issue, but the Bible is plain. According to Exodus chapter 20, a person who commits suicide is guilty of breaking the Third, Sixth, and Eighth Commandment. The Third Commandment says that we should have no other gods but the one true God, Yahweh. When a person commits suicide they have put something or someone above God; they have not trusted in the one true God, and they have silently stated that God is unable to deliver them from any kind of trouble or problems that they might be experiencing. They have also broken the Sixth Commandment which says that we should not kill or commit murder. The Bible does not specify if this murder is of self or another person. It just says we should not murder. The Eighth Commandment states that we should not steal, that is, take something that does not belong to us. As believers, our lives do not belong to us; they belong to Christ who paid the price for us with every drop of his sinless blood.

It is understandable how there could be situations when one would feel like taking his or her own life. I remember serving God with all of my heart at a time when God used me as his messenger. I was so close to God and I felt there was nothing I would withhold from him. I didn't even want an earthly husband. All I wanted was to serve God and live my life for him. Do I understand all of the events that ensued after this point? No, I do not, but God has finally given me peace. However, there were many excruciating trials I would have to endure before peace would take up residence.

I remember one morning, very early, I was praying for Sister R; she was married to Min. R who had other family at the church. Sister R had just had a baby and because of the aneurysm, she suffered a stroke. She was so young, only 25 years old. During my prayer that morning, God said that very day was Sister R's last day on earth. My heart broke and my soul was grieved. Then God revealed to me that Min. R would be my husband. I couldn't believe what I was hearing. That just couldn't be. God also said that I would have to keep that knowledge in my heart and to myself. I didn't know how to handle all of this. I was 13 years older than him. I had always been a person who was attracted to tall men; he was short. I couldn't resolve this within myself. I was about to try to find a loophole not to obey God, and in so doing, I was about pay the ultimate price.

Later that day, the pastor came over to my house. He said that Sister R had passed away, that the church secretary was out of town, and that he needed me to type up the bulletin for the memorial services. He gave me the format and the words and picture of a rose that Min. R wanted on the bulletin. God impressed upon me to write a poem for the occasion as a tribute to Sister R and encouragement for Min. R. However, I let my son read the poem instead of me because I knew Min. R would be emotional and I didn't want it to draw him closer to me. Also, my son lied, and tried to make Min. R believe that he wrote the poem. The word says, "Trust in the Lord with all of your heart and lean not unto your own understanding" (Proverbs 3:5). God knows that we'll mess it up every time. According to God's plan, the poem was supposed to draw Min. R close to me. One obedient thing I did was to invite him to come to my house sometime for Spaghetti dinner. He consented. However, this never happened. There were more events that I did not understand.

In spite of everything, Min. R and I became friends. He was looking for a job and asked me to type up his resume. I made the mistake of inadvertently insulting his ego. It was not intentional, but this was mistake number 507. What can I say; it's a gift ☺ I also noticed something odd. Sister S had been engaged to Min. R's cousin. I believe I heard that this was no longer the case. I saw how Sister S and Min. R acted around each other, and I knew what was coming. Min. R had confided in me that he wanted to become an elder but the pastor was dragging his feet. He told me how another minister friend of his had married a woman whose father was a bishop and the minister friend was now an elder. Sister S's grandfather was a bishop. When God puts two people together, I believe God tells the man and the woman the same thing. Somehow, I believe Min. R knew the truth, but he, along with I, did not want to receive it. God was trying to work out something in both of us; we had a great deal in common. Also, I discovered that I was older than him in years, but he was older than me in the Lord. God told me to join the choir. Min. R was the president of the choir and he played the keyboard. Instead of obeying God, I left the church and wrote Min. R a letter, telling him everything God had showed me, even the prophecies about God taking away a child, that the child would not see its first birthday. I said some negative things about the pastor that he and I had both talked about. In my disobedience and ignorance, I guess I thought I would never see him again because I left the church. However, God would eventually send me back.

Of course, Min. R and Sister S were engaged to be married. Min. R gave the letter to his mother who was a missionary in the church. During prayer time one morning, I spoke in tongues and interpreted. She, in anger, said before the whole church, that I was doing things in malice and that I was evil. This broke my heart and I sobbed like a child. I told them I never tried to hurt anyone. The pastor consoled me. Another time, this same missionary announced before the church that Sister S and Min. R were put together by God. She said that Sister S was destined to be the mother of Min. R's child by Sister R who had passed away. Min. R's sister also testified how the baby would go to no one except Sister S. I couldn't understand her saying this, because it was just after the time I had been babysitting Min. R's child in church and his sister later told me that the baby had been so quiet that she didn't even know I had him. Even though I knew what the missionary said was not true,

I said nothing the whole time. I didn't think it was possible, but things got worse after this.

Min. R let his mother read the letter I'd written. I had never felt so betrayed in my life. I and Min. R were called into the pastor's office. Min. R was angry and the pastor said that Min. R demanded an apology. I could not look at Min. R but I apologized to the both of them. I wanted to die. I couldn't stop sobbing during church services for a week after this. I told another missionary that I wanted to die. She, the pastor, and one of the deaconesses reminded me that I had so much to live for: my children. I didn't want to hurt my children; I just wanted the hurt to go away. I remember driving home from a temporary job in Chandler where I was told my services were no longer needed, although the assignment had not ended. I felt so low, such overwhelming sorrow, and such pity for myself. I felt as though God had let me down after everything I'd done in serving him. I let go of the steering wheel. I felt that the car would go wherever it wanted and my death would be an accident. God told me to put my hands back on the wheel because he and I would know the truth and that it would not be an accident in his eyes. Reluctantly, I complied. Guess what? I survived – not death, but life.

I'm sorry to say that the prophecies came true. Min. R and Sister R married and had a child on two separate occasions that was still born, that is, did not see its first birthday. Eventually they did have a child but years later they divorced. I had seen their divorce in a vision, but I had learned my lesson and did not share anything with anyone again when God instructed me not to do so. It's strange because before the divorce, I supported both Min. R and his wife in their ministry, visited them, and prayed for them. His wife was pregnant. I prayed for their marriage and for the child to be healthy. They had a little girl. Also, while over my house one day prior to this, Min. R confided in me about the Lord telling him that he would be a bishop. His wife had gone to the car to get something for the baby. I asked him if he saw himself being 50 years old as a bishop. He said that God had told him this. He became a bishop before the age of 50. I never saw him again after that, but I found out that he was engaged at one time but the woman called it off. His father passed away, his sister's marriage failed, his mother left the church and moved away and his ex-wife's family and his were always at odds. I prayed for all of them.

I went through what David and our Lord Jesus Christ (Yahoshua) went through. The same thing many of God's people have gone through. I was betrayed by a friend: we took sweet counsel together and we went into the house of God together; he was not an enemy (I could have borne this); he was a friend. Like David, I wanted wings like a dove to fly me away. (Psalm 55:6-14) I wanted to get away from the pain and agony. Like Christ, I wanted the cup to be taken away from me; I did not want to drink this bitterness. (Matthew 26:42) The death would be the spiritual death of friendship. However, Like David but unlike Christ, I caused my own pain and anguish due to my disobedience. God's word is to be followed completely and to the letter. Sometimes, it is to be followed in spite of our own understanding. I felt that I was not "telling" anyone about the letter if I "wrote" it down. God will not be mocked. I suffered because of my own ignorance and disobedience. The experience and the pain made me stronger. I learned the hard way that God is sovereign. Who are we that we should undermine his authority, his statues, and his judgment? He knows everything from beginning to end. He knows what we need, when we need it, and why we need it. It takes courage and trust in God to keep living and to keep going and to keep serving him in spite of our disappointments. Psalm 30:5 says, "For his anger endureth but a moment; in his favour is life: weeping may endure for a night, but joy cometh in the morning."

God, forgive me for even allowing the thought of suicide to enter my mind. Forgive me for disobeying you. You, and you along, know what it best for me. Help me to stop relying on my own understanding and to put my total and complete trust in you. I surrender my life into your hands. I commit myself to your spirit. Amen

The Best Grant of Immunity

"But he was wounded for our transgressions, he was bruised for our iniquities: the chastisement of our peace was upon him; and with his stripes we are healed." Isaiah 53:5

Life is in the blood. We're kept alive by this fluid made of tiny cells that die and are replaced every day by new ones. The average heart beats about 100,000 times a day. Approximately 70 ml (.07 ounces) of blood is pumped from the left ventricle during each heartbeat, which amounts to about 7,000 liters of blood each day. God created this interdependent system to keep us alive each day. Food, water, and air provide the necessary nutrients to ensure that the blood we produce is good and pure. It's all a matter of what we consume or what we allow to consume us.

Life could not exist without blood, but what happens when our blood is contaminated? So many diseases exist due to contamination of the blood. Since God created mankind, is omnipotent, is omnipresent, is omniscient, and has been with us throughout every age, he knows what is best for us and what the future holds. His laws are not harsh or burdensome when considered from this point of view. They exist to protect us and to keep us safe. We may not understand everything but history and present events continue to make us aware of God's all-knowing protective care.

When I was growing up it seemed that the most that could and did happen to people who had sex outside of marriage and/or unprotected sex is the woman ended up pregnant and sometimes the man or woman contracted a sexually transmitted disease. I remember when I was 18 and with my ex-husband, I had a doctor appointment due to what I thought was another yeast infection. How appalled and shocked I was to learn that I had gonorrhea. I couldn't believe it. I only had sex with my husband, no one else. The answer was easy though not easily accepted: my ex-husband had been unfaithful and had passed the disease onto me. When confronted, he lied and said that I must have given it to him. Not only did he not admit to it, but I learned that men have symptoms and early signs so they can get treated early. However, it is possible for women to go past the point of no return without knowing they are infected. In other words, they can die from the disease. This meant that my ex-husband was willing to risk my death rather than admit his sin.

Today, sex can literally kill you, thanks to the HIV virus and the ensuing A.I.D.S. It is evident that this disease was man-made; however, it has its direct inception from the wicked one. Everything God created, the Devil has a counterfeit. God created the important T-cell. According to the medical dictionary, the T-cell is a type of white blood cell that is vital to the immune system and is at the core of "adaptive immunity" which is the system that tailors the body's immune response to a specific virus or bacterium. It is said that the T cells are like "soldiers who search out and destroy the targeted invaders." The HIV virus disguises itself as a T-cell and infiltrates the ranks. They, like sheep in wolves clothing, become one of them. They become the tares sown among the good wheat. The body's immune system is destroyed.

No matter what lies are spread today, A.I.D.S. was most prevalent among the gay community. Most homosexuals, like most people who are in sin, engaged in sex with multiple partners. This type of anal sex tears the tender lining and makes one vulnerable to becoming infected with HIV. People who are in sin and depraved, are not discriminating with whom and with what they have sex. Some people call themselves bi-sexual and have sex with both sexes. Some have sex with animals. There are both natural and spiritual consequences for sin. I've had an uncle, two male cousins, two ministers, and friend who all died from A.I.D.S. All of them were black males except for one who was a black female. Two of them died of A.I.D.S. due to intravenous drug use: male cousin and female friend. The others had been in homosexual lifestyles. I cried with all of them and mourned with them. All of them accepted Christ into their lives before they died and had renounced the life of homosexuality.

In today's promiscuous society, there are not many unmarried virgins. However, there are some. Television and movies portray them as freaks and their behavior as socially unacceptable. Many say there is something wrong with them, especially if they are male. They are in very good company: Jesus, Paul, and Jeremiah to name a few. Some are obedient to the word and do not have sex outside of marriage. Some choose not to marry at all. They have the gift of celibacy. It is one of the spiritual gifts and only God is able to keep them. The Bible tells us to be content in whatever state we find ourselves: rich, poor, married, or single. (Philippians 4:12) God is able to supply our every need. The Hebrew Israelites were required at one time to present a lamb, goat, or dove as a blood sacrifice for their sins. The animal had to be without spot or wrinkle. It had to be pure. The blood could not be contaminated. (Number 19:2) Such was the life of Christ. He was without spot or wrinkle. He was pure and without the contamination of sin. He was the last and perfect lamb. (John 1:29) His blood covered our sins and washed away the sentence of death that was upon us. To maintain this pure blood, we need only continue in obedience to the word of God. God's immutable, infallible, and grace-filled word is the only thing that will keep us both physically and spiritually. "In the beginning was the word and the word was with God, and the word was God" (John 1:1). Jesus Christ (Yahoshua) and the Bible which foretells and represents him, is our T-cell. This is the core of our "adaptive immunity." Only when we are changed into his image can we search out and destroy invaders. Old things are passed away, and behold all things become new. (2 Corinthians 5:17)

> *Lord, I know that all sexual sin leads to death, both physically and spiritually. Help me to forego what is popular and socially-acceptable and to adhere to your word. I confess all the evil within my heart and soul and my past evil deeds. Lead me in the paths of righteousness for your names sake, anoint my head with oil so that my cup runs over, and let me dwell in your house forever. Amen*

A Helpmate for All Seasons

"For we are members of his body, of his flesh, and of his bones. For this cause shall a man leave his father and mother, and shall be joined unto his wife, and they two shall be one flesh." Ephesians 5:30-31

Based on the number of divorces each year, it appears most people fall in love with the idea of marriage rather than the person they are going to marry. They know each other probably for all of two weeks and decide this is the person with whom I want to spend the rest of my life. Most of them are so starry eyed or so anxious to get to the honeymoon that they don't really listen or take careful thought to the vows they are making. There are traditional vows and non-traditional vows. The most popular: "I, (name), take you (name), to be my (wife/husband), to have and to hold from this day forward, for better or for worse, for richer, for poorer, in sickness and in health, to love and to cherish; from this day forward until death do us part." Another popular vow: "I, (name), take you, (name), to be my lawfully wedded (husband/wife), my constant friend, my faithful partner and my love from this day forward. In the presence of God, our family and friends, I offer you my solemn vow to be your faithful partner in sickness and in health, in good times and in bad, and in joy as well as in sorrow. I promise to love you unconditionally, to support you in your goals, to honor and respect you, to laugh with you and cry with you, and to cherish you for as long as we both shall live." Unfortunately, most of them discover after about a year that either they or their spouses are going to live just a little too long.

According to Ecclesiastes 5:5, it is better not to make a vow before the Lord than to make a vow and not pay. Some of the vows used to include the word "obey," but because of women opposition, some have opted to omit the word. However, the word "obey" and the word "love" are the only two words of the vows that are from the Bible. The rest of the popular vows *are* based on Scripture, however. A person is to cling to his or her spouse and forsake all others, including mother and father. It is s easy to say the words that you will love and cherish your spouse even when that person is sick or poor, especially when things are going well and everyone is healthy, happy, and opening wedding gifts. What we fail to remember is that God instituted marriage when he gave Eve to Adam. They each would get someone to complement them, not complete them. We look for a spouse to fulfill us and to be everything to us. This is an almost impossible order for fallen mankind.

I remember when my friends Linda and Tommy were getting married. I enjoyed their wedding so much because everything in the ceremony symbolized the true meaning of marriage: the church, the bride of Christ, uniting with its bridegroom, Christ. Ephesians 5:21 says, "Submitting yourselves one to another in the fear of God." Sometimes people miss this part. It is not just the wife who submits. Both the wife and the husband are to submit to one another. Also, it is not just submission, but a loving and willing submission in the fear of God. As the church is subject unto Christ, so the wife is to submit to her husband. As Christ loved the church and gave his life for it, so the husband is to love his wife. Before a person marries, he or she should prayerfully consider whether or not this is a vow they are committed to keeping.

Needless to say, the marriage vows are sacred oaths before the Lord. They are not based on the actions of the other person, but on our specific commitment to God and to our spouse. They are also not based on events that happen. The vows serve as a contract, that when broken by either party, leaves that person guilty before God. It is up to the offending party to prayerfully seek God before making a decision to terminate. However, it was never God's vision for it to be so. (Matthew 5:31-32) This is why couples need to be first submitted and committed to Christ. They need to spend time, a great amount of time, getting to know and interact with the person before they get married. You do not have to live with someone to get to know them in various situations. You need to know their faults and whether or not you can live with those faults. It is a waste of time and a disservice for couples to be on their "best behavior" all of the time. We are imperfect human beings. We are sinners saved by grace. (Ephesians 2:8) We have gases and elements that emanate from the many holes in our bodies. We have to intake nutrients and expel wastes in order to survive. We get tired, sleepy, hungry, angry, and may not look too good when we wake up after 7 or 8 hours of slumber. As we age, our hair and our teeth may fall out. Our once vigor bodies may slow down, bend over, bulge forth, and give way to gravity – all of this before "death do us part." We have to see past the objects of sexual desire that TV and movies tell us is so important. We may end up with more month than money. We may end up with more money than time to spend with loved ones. Our interests may change. We will not always agree. We may learn more and we may grow more, and our partners may not. Other people, like children, friends, and in-laws may invade our honeymoon years. Also, illness and financial setbacks may interfere with our temporal plans of paradise.

What a mess! Taking all the foregoing into consideration, how in the world can anyone be expected to keep these marriage vows? First, through prayer on a daily basis, remembering those vows made to each other and in the presence and fear of God. Remember the sacrifice Christ made by his life and death. Remember Jesus' words in the Garden of Gethsemane that his will be subject to the God's will (Matthew 26:42). Remember that your marriage represents the union of Christ with his church. Remember that the Word says that where two or three are gathered in his name that he dwells in the midst of them. (Matthew 18:20) Remember that we are all different and that we can agree to disagree and still love each other. Remember that self must die daily and be submitted to the Word of God. Remember, that as a believer, your life and first witness must be to your spouse. This is why God has instructed us not to be unequally yoked with unbelievers. (2 Corinthians 6:14) Remember that you cannot change anyone; you can only change yourself. God commanded the wife to obey, that is, submit to her husband as the church submits to Christ.

God commanded the husband to love and cherish his wife and be willing to give his life for her as Christ did for us, his church. What is so amazing is that you find marriages where both the husband and the wife both obey and submit and both love and cherish each other. Why? Because they know that everything they do they do not as unto men, but unto God (Colossians 3:23).

> *Father, my marriage vows represent my vows to you. Forgive me when my words, my thoughts, or my actions are contrary to this. Help me to see my spouse the way you do. Help me to remember and never forget your sacrifice for me and for my spouse. Help me to trust that you will meet our every need, in sickness and in health, for richer or for poorer, in good times and in not so good times, until death do us part. Amen*

Those Are Fighting Words

He that is slow to anger is better than the mighty; and he that ruleth his spirit than he that taketh a city." Proverbs 16:32

What is it that makes us angry? Is there an appropriate time for anger? How should we act in these instances? People have killed in anger and people have been killed by someone else's anger. Wars have been fought that originated out of anger. Friendships have died out of misplaced and misguided anger. How many times have you heard someone caution: "Don't say something you'll regret"? Yet, this warning goes unheeded. We get angry because someone has insulted us and hurt our pride and ego. We get angry because of injustice and oppression against us, loved ones, or others who we believe do not deserve to be treated as such. Some people have a shorter fuse than others. When a person is angry, they are no longer thinking rationally.

Anger can be controlled and expressed properly. The Bible says to be angry but don't sin. (Ephesians 4:26) The apostle James warns us to be quick to listen, slow to speak, and slow to get angry. (James 1:19) Our anger can never make things right in God's sight. King David tells us in Psalm 37:8 to turn from rage and not to envy others because it only leads to harm, both ours and others. King Solomon tells us in the book of Ecclesiastes not to be quick-tempered because anger is the friend of fools. The book of Proverbs is full of advice to keep away from being angry and short-tempered and that we earn esteem by overlooking wrongs.

Of course, all of this is better said than done. I used to get so angry with what I believed was stupidity and obstinate customer service representatives or restaurant workers. It didn't matter if it was in person or on the phone. I ran into people who never thought for themselves. If I made a request of someone out of the ordinary or had an unusual situation, I would get the standard, "It's against company policy" or "We've always done it this way." Most of the time, I would end up talking with their manager or supervisor. I have been so angry with my children when they were disobedient or obstinate. I have hit them out of anger, spanked them out of anger, and regretted it later. It took me awhile before I would no longer be led by anger and my emotions, but I allowed God to be in control of the situation. I realized that when my manner was different, so was theirs, and I got a lot more accomplished.

Modern psychology tells us today to "express your anger" and "let your emotions out." They believe it's good for the soul. However, we know that the world's philosophy is contrary to that of the Bible. We should be angry with injustice and with sin. Jesus took a whip and overturned the tables of the money changers in the Temple. He did not whip the people; he hit the ground. They knew he was angry with what they were doing: desecrating God's house of prayer and making it into a "den of thieves" (Matthew 21:13). We should remember to make sure people know we are angry with their behavior but that we still love them. This is not easy to do when we believe we have been slighted, wronged, or insulted. Self gets in the way of rational judgment. If we did as the Word says that true love is supposed to do: think on the things of others, remain patient and kind, refrain from being puffed up and arrogant, and take no thought of how we are wronged, anger would not be allowed to take up residence within our hearts and minds (1 Corinthians 13). Anger would not be allowed to smolder and fester until it evolves into a cancerous disease that invades and destroys the soul and sometimes, physically kills the body. It doesn't matter if the person who has wronged you is living or non living. If they are living and accessible, we can go to our knees for that person and the situation. We can then go to that person in love and tell them how we felt when they did what they did. The goal is restoration and reconciliation, not guilt and accusation. Sometimes we're received well and sometimes not. However, you have fulfilled your duty as a person of God. Leave them in the hands of Almighty Yah. They have to answer to him and not to us. If the person is not living and/or not accessible, we must still go to our knees and purpose in our hearts to forgive that person. When you learn to put everything into perspective by focusing on the sacrifice of Jesus on the cross, how he lived, and how he forgave with his dying breath those who crucified him, how can we not forgive someone who has wronged us or someone we care about? It is not something we can do in and of ourselves, but we "can do all things through Christ who strengthens us" (Philippians 4:13).

> My Lord and Savior, I know you are angry with sin, injustice, and oppression every day. I know the ultimate price you paid and gave your earthly life. Help me to control my anger so that sin does not reign within me. Help me to remember that you will conquer my enemies. I, on the other hand, must conquer self. Amen

We Shall Overcome – Our Fear

For God hath not given us the spirit of fear; but of power, and of love, and of a sound mind." 2 Timothy 1:7

From the time we wake up in the morning to the time we lie back down to go to sleep at night, there is one thing that can debilitate us more than anything else: fear. It can even deprive us of much needed sleep. Fear, along with its twin, worry, comes in so many different forms and they have their basis in Maslow's hierarchy of needs. People worry about and fear not having enough food, water, and shelter. They fear not being safe from the elements, from wild animals, from thieves, from murderers, from anyone and anything that threatens their safety. They fear being alone, they fear crowds, they fear not having someone to love, they fear their loved one leaving them, and they fear what other people will think of them. They fear not reaching their accomplishments, not being successful and admired by others, and they fear not reaching their highest potential. Whether the fear and worry is warranted or not, it can still be debilitating.

Every time I have to give a presentation or speak in front of a group of people, fear comes upon me. It is an instinctual part of human nature. There will be one of two responses: flight or fight. You can choose to run away or fight through your fears. I pray during the planning and delivery of my presentation, no matter if I'm speaking or teaching a lesson. I remind myself that I'm prepared and that God is with me every step of the way. I remind myself that Christ said he'll never leave me nor forsake me and that he is with me always. I remind myself that I can do all things through Christ who strengthens me. This calms me and then I forget about self as I start to focus on the people who are in the audience or classroom. I focus on the material that I am to present or to teach. My fear and worry turn to purpose and direction. My focus is no longer on what they will think of me; my focus is now on what I can do to help them. After all, this is the reason I am making the presentation or teaching in the first place. I am the messenger, God is with me, I have a message to deliver, and I have a duty to fulfill. Even if I make mistakes and everything does not go according to my expert plans, I remember that all is not lost. Both I and the audience have learned something.

A wise man, Franklin Roosevelt, once said, "We have nothing to fear except fear itself." However, the Bible tells us that we have nothing to fear. Jesus told us not to worry about food, what we will eat, or what we will wear. He assured us that God feeds the birds of the air, clothes the lilies of the field, and that nothing goes without his care and notice (Luke 12:29-32). Isaiah, a prophet called of God, voiced his fears before God. God reassured him to the point that in Isaiah 43:1-3, Isaiah assures us not to be afraid because God has ransomed us, that he has called us by name and we belong to him, that when we go through deep waters and rivers of difficulty, we will not drown, that when we walk through the fire of oppression, we will not be burned nor consumed. Paul reminds us that not even death, life, angels, or demons can separate us from the love of God (Romans 8:37-39). David reminds us in the 23rd Psalm that even when we walk through the valley of the shadow of death, we do not have to be afraid because not only is the Lord close beside us but his rod and his staff protects us, his precious sheep.

When my grandmother was dying of cancer, I was either 8 or 9 years old. She had been a maid to a doctor in Arizona who, despite her continual ailment, could find nothing wrong with her. It was not until she moved to California and consulted another doctor that she was diagnosed with uterine cancer that had advanced to the point that it was terminal. Many times she would be screaming in pain. I remember asking her what was wrong and she told me she was dying. I told her I was afraid. She told me to read the 23rd Psalm and to memorize it. I did this. I realized that day that my grandmother may have been in terrible excruciating pain, but she definitely had no fear. She knew she could face God on judgment day because she had been washed in the precious blood of the lamb. She had been reconciled to God and now belonged to him.

Some of us will sleep before Christ returns; some of us will remain until that time. We may experience the time of great tribulation. Even if this is the case, the apostle John, in Revelation 2:10 encourages us not to fear what we are to suffer. He says that the Devil will throw some of us into prison and put our faith to the test. Yes, some of us may have to seal our testimony with our blood, just as so many of the apostles, prophets, and many people of God all over the world today. However, as John exhorts us, if we remain faithful even when facing death, God will give us the crown of life. Our natural man does not want to die; this is normal. It's called self-preservation and built into each of us. However, when our spiritual man takes over and we die to self, through faith we know and trust that God will quicken our mortal bodies, give us new spiritual bodies, and that we will reign throughout eternity and finally see face-to-face the one who gave his all that we might have all.

Father, with your help, I vow this day to overcome any fear of people, of things, of situations, of death, or even of self. Help me to focus on what I have to give to others and my duty to you. May I always speak the truth in love. May I always act with holy boldness in all that I do. Amen

---

Show Them the Money

He who is hard on the poor puts shame on his Maker; but he who has mercy on those who are in need gives him honour."
Proverbs 14:31

I am amazed every time I read articles about the rich and famous. Of course, not everyone who is rich is famous and not everyone who is famous is rich. I read stories about celebrities such as Oprah, who is worth a few billion dollars, Jerry Seinfeld who not only has close to a billion dollars, but he collects cars and houses all of them within a 4-story car garage. Anyone who has tried to find a parking space at an event and had to drive up two or three levels knows the multitude of cars this entails. Of course, this would mean he has to either pay people to service and take care of these cars for him or he has to spend time doing it himself, which, even if it's a hobby, is highly unlikely. I hear stories of people winning close to $300 million dollars in the lottery, sometimes because they happen to buy a ticket by accident. What's even more appalling is when I learn that a lot of these people are not only broke or nearly broke within a few years, but they describe how the money was a "burden" or detail the troubles they encountered. I heard of a woman who had struggled raising her two children by herself and had to declare bankruptcy. She was now employed with a correctional facility where she's had feces thrown into her face by some of the inmates. She meant to buy one of the regular lottery tickets as she said she does every six months. However, she accidentally bought a Mega Million Lottery Ticket – and won $40 million dollars. Okay, so the good old IRS, a non-government, unconstitutional, for-profit entity, claims $10 million of this in taxes. What was even more amazing was that she said she didn't know what to do with that much money and she will not quit her job because her employers have been so good to her.

These are just a few. There are even so-called believers, even preachers of the gospel of Christ, who have more wealth than they could image. Even though I know people, like Oprah, Seinfeld, and others who are wealthy, both believers and nonbelievers, donate monies to help others, I still can't imagine how anyone can live in mansions and castles, with more rooms than they could possibly need. I don't understand people owning 15 closets of clothing and still claiming they have nothing to wear. I don't understand athletes with hundreds of millions of dollars owning hundreds of pairs of shoes when they only have two feet. The reason I don't understand any of this is because there are people who have no shoes. There are people who are literally eating dirt every day. There are children who don't know what it's like to sleep on a nice comfortable bed. There are enough resources and enough money on this planet to make sure that everyone has everything they need, not necessarily everything they want. Healthy food, water, shelter, safety are not luxuries. They are necessities. God knew this. Everything he created he said it was good. He didn't put a price tag on anything. He gave it freely to all us.

Since the beginning of time and throughout history, we hear of those who have killed and pillaged to control and claim territory. In other words, they took what they wanted and if others wanted to do the same, usually they were killed. This goes on even to this day. Once they controlled all of the resources they set up government and laws to make sure no one else would be able to do what they did. This is how they controlled the masses. Others who would need what the dictators had stolen would now have to work to get worthless pieces of paper (currency) to purchase what God had already given to man freely: food, water, shelter, and land. None of the governments have worked because none of them are what God intended. Capitalism, Communism, and Socialism are all different sides of the same coin. There is, even today, enough land and resources for everyone, yes, for all 6 billion people in the world. So why are people starving? Because of greed and selfishness.

Everything that Jesus warned us about: the lust of the flesh, the lust of the eye, and the pride of life, are the very evils that have crushed our earthly economy and left us spiritually bankrupt. Jesus had to fast 40 days and 40 nights to be strengthened against these same temptations. He was tested and tried and emerged victoriously. (Matthew 4:1-11) The spirits of greed and selfishness are concoctions from the Devil himself. He, once called Lucifer, the bright and morning star, rebelled against a holy and just God. Lucifer was cast down along with a third of the fallen angels. It is they who control this world and its evil and unjust system. This spirit has pervaded every facet. The spirit of Antichrist has darkened the minds of so many. Human life is worth nothing to them. Their consciences have been seared and they have been blinded with the quest for what they believe is success, fame, glory, and wealth. They know that "he who controls the gold controls the world," and they are intent on doing just that: controlling the world. There is no compassion in their hearts for others. In fact, some of them delight in knowing that they have taken away everything from others and they, they alone, are without equal monetarily. They are like little boys struggling, fighting, and killing to come away with all of the marbles in their bags.

Jesus says we live in this world but we are not of this world. He reminds us not to worry about anything, but to take one day at a time. People who amass more than they could possibly use in one lifetime claim they are doing so to leave a legacy and to build security for their children and their children. However, wise Solomon, a man of God without equal in wealth, warned us that it is all "vanity," which translated means "nothingness." Most people with extreme wealth are so consumed with trying to make more money and finding ways to protect their wealth, they don't really take time to enjoy their lives. I used to envy them; now I pity them. I am reminded of the story of the rich young ruler whose sole goal in life was to build additional facilities to house his assets. We can liken this to the filthy rich who have countless Swiss and offshore bank accounts containing dollar amounts that would seem unreal to most of us. The same thing God said to the rich man in the Bible story is the same thing God says to the wealthy today: "You fool, this night your soul is required." (Luke 12:20).

My Lord and Savior, if at any time the spirits of greed and selfishness attempt to take up residence within me, I pray that you root them out. Forgive me when I fail to remember that everything belongs to you and you alone. Help me to exercise true love that says, "Yes, I am my brother's keeper." Amen

Pulling Them Out of the Fire

"Therefore said he unto them, The harvest truly is great, but the labourers are few: pray ye therefore the Lord of the harvest, that he would send forth labourers into his harvest." Luke 10:2

Statistics show that 150,000 people die every day. It always amazes me how you can be here one day and gone the next. Life is so precious, so fleeting, and so short. I was just thinking about an individual with whom I'd interacted through the Dept. of Education. In fact, she was the Program Administrator for the Adult Literacy Program in Yuma and served as our distance learning collaborative partners. She had been a bit overweight. I didn't know she had moved from Arizona to Maine. We received word that she died of a heart attack shortly after attending her father's funeral in Arizona. I was grieved. I did not know her that well, but I had an opportunity to share my faith with her and did not. I still wonder if she was saved.

I remember a student named Randy who was a resident of the juvenile detention center where I used to work. He asked me after class one day if I understood the Psalms in the Bible. I told him that I did. He asked me if I would explain them to him. I didn't take the time right then because we were told we needed to make sure the residents kept to their schedules to get to lunch on time. However, it was not physical food he needed; he needed spiritual food. I had intended to make it a priority with him, but never did. He was released a month later and was shot and killed.

I'm sure we all have such scenarios. As saved people of God, we know that there is nothing more important than our eternal salvation, so why does witnessing to the lost get relegated to a low level on our list of priorities? Have we become too complacent or sidetracked by our day to day activities? Maybe we lack the one thing that is needed: compassion. There is a story that is told about a firefighter who was new on the job. He was the first one to receive a call about a fire nearby. He was the first one on the scene. He did have a fire truck and the life-saving equipment with him; however, he sat there and waited for more firefighters to arrive. Because he felt he had to wait, he put on his headphones and listened to music while we waited. In the meantime, a family of five died. The father jumped to his death while clutching the two smallest children. The mother and oldest child were burned alive. By now you're probably beside yourself and angry with this firefighter. How could anyone be so insensitive? It was his duty to do everything he could, regardless of how inadequate or unprepared he felt. He was the only one there. Obviously, the unfaithful firefighter should be punished.

It's easy to see the unfaithfulness and lack of responsibility on the part of others, but what about us? Do we, like the firefighter, fail to do everything on our part, despite our feelings of inadequacy or unpreparedness, to save the lost from the fires of Hell? Do we wait for others who we feel are more experienced to show up while the lost are burning up in their sin and jumping to their deaths? Do we silence their cries for help, whether spoken or unspoken? What should be our punishment for our unfaithfulness? It is a fact that the lost will die in their sins, but God will hold us accountable, and their blood will be on our hands.

Jesus' command was to "go ye into all the world and preach the gospel to every creature" (Mark 16:15). This commission was not given just to the church pastor or to those designated as the church evangelists. When Jesus said "go you" he was talking directly to his disciples. Everyone who is a disciple of the Lord Jesus Christ has this responsibility. We are not to be content with our church anniversaries, pastoral anniversaries, district meetings, and other countless activities that have nothing to do with our true purpose as the church. If we think we are fulfilling the great commission, we need to think again and check this against scripture. Jesus said that the harvest is plentiful but the workers were few. He prayed that the God, the Lord of the harvest, would send workers. (Matthew 9:37-38) We are the workers, all of us, not just those with man-made titles. These titles mean nothing to God. We have a responsibility, a duty, to seek and save those who are lost. If you feel inadequate, you're in good company. Men like Gideon, Isaiah, Amos, Moses, and the apostle Paul all felt the same way. In each case, God promised to be with them, to teach them what to say, and to prepare them. We need only answer the call. We are those who plant and water, but it is God who will give the increase (1 Corinthians 3:7).

> *My God, the author and finisher of my faith, forgive me if I have neglected my duty in seeking to save the lost. Please help me to cultivate true compassion that stems from true love. Help me to remember that you are with me, that I am never alone, that I need only do my part, and you will surely do the rest.   Amen*

No More False Converts

"And he said unto him, Why callest thou me good? there is none good but one, that is, God: but if thou wilt enter into life, keep the commandments."
Matthew 19:17

September 11, 2011 will commemorate the 10ᵗʰ year anniversary of that awful event which we still refer to as 9-11. It was a time of distress and represented its call numbers; it was a call for help. Everyone in the country was in an uproar over the devastation of the Twin Towers going down, planes hijacked by terrorists, the White House threatened, and the hundreds of lives lost. Even though it was later suspected that our government orchestrated the entire events from beginning to end, it affected the very essence of our existence and made us focus on our mortality. Everyone was praying and church attendance rose higher than it had ever been. Of course, as time wanes and people do not feel another attack may be impending, their "religious conversion" wanes right along with it. Once again, they feel safe and secure.

Doesn't this sound like most of the so-called spiritual conversions? In one year, there were around 290,000 people in the United States who gave their lives to Christ; however, a year later, only 14,000 could be accounted for. We call them backsliders; however, in reality, they were never truly converted in the first place. They are what we call children of "modern evangelism." Modern evangelism allows people to come to God for the wrong reason. They tell the lost soul that Jesus loves them and wants them to have a wonderful life. Now it is true that Jesus loves them, but what usually happens when the person comes to Christ? Well, the Bible tells us that all who will live godly will suffer persecution. (2 Timothy 3:12) It does not say that we'll have a wonderful life. In fact, it says just the opposite. It does not promise earthly wealth, earthly happiness, but inner peace and eternal joy. When people encounter trials and tribulations rather than the "wonderful life" the witness had promised them, they become discouraged and disillusioned; more times than not, they fall away from the faith.

Jesus, the master teacher and master evangelist, knew how to reach the lost. He knew how to circumvent the intellect and target the conscience, the seat of the knowledge of right and wrong. If you ask most people if they are a good person, of course they will answer in the affirmative. When the man came to Jesus and he said "Good Master," Jesus told him, "Why do you call me good, there is none good but God." He then told him that if he wanted to enter into life that he should keep the commandments. (Matthew 19:17) Remember, Jesus did not come to destroy the law but to fulfill the law. Paul said that the only way he would know sin was by the law. The law serves as a mirror to reveal to us how sinful and dirty we really are. (Romans 7:7) This is what Jesus used when the man came to him and asked him what he must do to have eternal life. When Jesus told him to keep the law, the man asked which ones. Jesus named only a few of them that pertain to our relationship to our fellow man: do not murder, do not steal, do not lie, and do not commit adultery. The man stated he had done all of this from his youth, but Jesus knew what was in man and he tested the man's true commitment. He told the man to sell all he had and come and follow him (Jesus). The man went away sorrowful because he had great possessions, that is, his heart and commitment were not right. (Matthew 19:20-22)

We know we are saved by grace through faith. The law cannot save us; it just lets us know that we need a savior. The law does not condemn us; it just leaves us guilty before a just and merciful God. A person may be sick and need a physician, but if the person is not convinced of his or her illness, it will be pointless to offer the person the needed remedy. If a person is not convinced that he or she has broken a law and has a fine to pay, it will seem ridiculous and absurd to tell the person that his or her fine has been paid. In both cases, the individuals may humor you but they will have nothing to sustain them. They will have no foundation on which to stand. The same is true for the sinner. If he or she is not convinced that he or she is guilty of sin, it is ridiculous to tell the person Jesus loves him or her and died to pay for his or her sins. The Bible says to give the law to the proud and grace to the humble. (James 4:6)

It takes the conviction of the powerful two-edged sword of the spirit to break up and cut through the fallow ground of the heart to prepare the heart for the grace-filled gospel. Just as the needle makes way for the thread, so does the law make way for the good news. Once a person is convicted of his or her own personal sin that has made the person an enemy of God, a condition that leaves the person guilty and worthy of punishment whereby he or she is facing the fires of Hell, then and only then is the person ready for the cure, for the solution, for the good new that Jesus paid the ultimate price and has made a way for him or her to be saved. This knowledge of a loving savior will drive the person to his or her knees to repent, to seek God with his or her whole heart, to want to attend church, and to want to seek the scriptures on his or her own. When a person is converted, we don't have to lead the person in the "sinner's prayer" because he or she has submitted himself or herself to God and is being led by him.

Almighty God, I want to seek and save the lost the way Jesus did. Help me to allow your light of your law to dispel and reveal the dark places of the mind and heart of sinners. May I never be afraid to call sin by its true name: transgression of the law. May I remember that none of us are good and that even I need your word to be a lamp unto my feet so that while I find myself preaching to others that I do not become a castaway. Amen

I Feel Therefore I Am

"For I reckon that the sufferings of this present time are not worthy to be compared with the glory which shall be revealed in us."
Romans 8:18

God created man with five earthly senses: sight, hearing, smell, taste, and touch. In a great number of people, one or two senses may be heightened over the others. For example, I have poor eyesight, have a hearing impairment, and care barely walk straight most of the time, but my sense of taste is great and my sense of smell heightened far beyond what I desire at times. One sense heightened over the other is usually more tell-tale when a person is born with or loses the ability to see or hear. A blind person's sense of hearing and touch help compensate for the lack of sight. A deaf person's sense of sight helps compensate for the lack of hearing.   So basically, the senses are needed for functioning, protection, and serve as a form of communication.

Sometimes people associate and remember specific events in their lives based on these senses. The smell of popcorn may remind you of family get-togethers when you were a child. The sound of a bell ringing may remind you of your days in church school. When you see a rose it may remind you of the last gift you received on Valentine's Day. When you eat Butter Pecan Ice Cream it may remind you of the walks home with your best friend during your college years. When you put on a silk tie it may remind you of your wife's silk stockings on your wedding night. These are pleasant memories but the senses can also bring back unpleasant memories. The screeching sound of a car may remind you of your little sister's fatal car accident and you were unable to do anything to prevent it. When you see a Doberman it may remind you of when you were bitten by your neighbor's dog that got loose. When you eat Neapolitan Ice Cream it may remind you of the time you waited for a date who never showed up and never called, so you pigged out. The touch of a hand with hairy knuckles may bring that awful day when you were molested or raped.

These are called "negative markers" in our lives. Most of the time, we never get to the root of problems and identify these markers. Usually, we try to treat the symptoms by deadening one or more of the senses. How do we do this? With drugs, of course. It does not matter if the drug is termed "over-the-counter," "prescription" or "illegal," it is still harmful to the body. It is unnatural and with time not only will the body build-up immunity, but it will cause damaging effects to other parts of the body. We are a society that wants to feel good all of the time. We want to eliminate any and all indications of pain. I read a news article of a little 5-year-old named Ashlyn. She suffers from CIPA (Congenital Insensitivity to Pain with Anhidrosis), a rare disorder that makes her unable to feel pain. At first, most people think this would be great, except pain is the body's natural alarm system. You can easily burn your hand off or bleed to death because you had no warning signs. Your body would also be unable to cool itself because you have lost the ability to sweat. When you have a headache, the body is sending signals to the brain that something is wrong in the body. Instead of identifying and treating the root of the problem, we grab the first aspirin or Tylenol within reach.

Because we never get to the root of the problem, this learned behavior becomes habitual, and since the body builds up immunity and we must get back to the initial feeling of "nirvana," we either up the dosage or find a stronger and more "effective" drug. Is it any wonder that people become addicted to drugs, both over-the-counter, prescription, and illegal? Is it any wonder that people die from accidental overdose? My heart bleeds when I hear about people like Michael Jackson, Brittany Murphy, and Pete Ledger who overdosed. I am remembered about people like Elvis, Marilyn Monroe, and Billie Holiday. Were they saved when they died? Only God knows. These are celebrities, but what about the multitude we don't hear about by name but are merely represented by a statistic?

There is a saying, "No pain; no gain." However, it is absurd to think I am advocating masochism and that we should love pain. What I am advocating is the same thing the Bible advocates: allow pain to work for you. Let it be your guide, your warning system, that all is not well. Allow it to make you stronger. The apostle Paul is an example of one who suffered shipwreck, beatings, hunger, and imprisonment, to name just a few painful circumstances. However, he endured these things and more and he wrote the Book of Philippians, a book that encourages us to rejoice and be exceedingly glad (3:1; 4:4), a book that tells us to think on the things that are lovely, pure, true, and of good report (4:8). Paul wrote, rather dictated this to his scribe, during the time he was in chains. His body endured pain but his mind and spirit focused on the love of Christ and the sacrifice of Christ. He focused on the promise of the time when "this mortality will put on immortality," and "this corruptible will put on incorruptible" (I Corinthians 15:54). God will give us new spiritual bodies. We won't feel pain; we won't need to. There won't be anything else to threaten our eternal existence or our safety, and we will have direct and continual communication with God. (Revelation 22:3-5)

Lord God, the Great I AM, you created me a little lower than the angels. I know that everything within me works and operates with purpose. You have provided every natural herb I need to keep me healthy. You have supplied me with all that I need. However, I know that this corruptible life will bring disappointments, sorrows, pain, and suffering. Let the comfort of your word sustain me and help me to endure to the end. Amen

Code of Conduct

*"A wise son heareth his father's instruction: but a scorner
heareth not rebuke." Proverbs 13:1*

I have a cousin who is a celebrity athlete and married to a well-known actress. I remember how appalled I was to see them on the TV show, *Dr. Phil*, trying to get advice because they said they couldn't control their child. We live in a world today where unsaved parents will throw up their hands and say, "I've tried nothing and I'm all out of ideas." We have the best instruction book on this subject. The Bible says that "Foolishness is bound in the heart of a child but the rod of correction with drive it far from him" (Proverbs 22:15). Of course this doesn't mean to abuse your child. The "rod" in the Bible was the shepherd's rod that he used to gently, but sternly, to prod the sheep when they would stray and the staff would steer the sheep in the right direction. This was for their protection. In the same way, good parents will train and discipline their children. However, discipline and rebuke do not feel good. Because of this, a lot of parents have opted for the Dr. Spock philosophy which usually culminates into allowing your child to do whatever they want, whatever feels good to them, whatever agrees with their "spirit."

The problem is the Bible says that our spiritual natures are innately in opposition to God and his laws. (Romans 3:10-18) Children are innately foolish and disobedient and they must be trained and disciplined as is the case in everything in life. (Proverbs 22:15) People hire physical trainers to help them to discipline their bodies, whip it into shape, so they can either lose weight or maintain their current physiques. People hire consultants to tell them what they are doing wrong and why they are not achieving the results they want in life, whether it is business, financial, political, social, or educational. They are asking for training and seek discipline. However, a great number of these same individuals balk at God's training and discipline with respect to morality. In these situations they want to be free to do whatever feels good. Unfortunately, sexual assault feels good to a rapist; murder feels good to a serial killer, and stealing feels good to a professional thief. Usually, these are people who either never received parental training or who never allowed the training and discipline to take root within them, and therefore, chose the route of antisocial behavior and deviance.

When God used me as his prophet he told me I was his belt. He showed me that a father's belt has two uses: support (hold up his pants) and discipline. It was great when God used me to encourage and uplift others. I enjoyed writing poetry and songs to provide support to help others grow spiritually and to comfort them in times of trials and troubles. However, I did not like when I had to speak God's words of discipline, especially those words of impending trials and consequences for their disobedience. It took me a while to recover from my Jonah-complex. God chastens those that he loves. Parents who care anything at all about their children will discipline them. Parents don't enjoy this but they do realize it is necessary. Just as children need praise and hugs, they also need discipline and hard words. Even though I did not like and appreciate it at the time, I realized it was the teachers who were most hard on me that taught me the most. I still remember their lessons and have learned a great deal from them. It is said that "Discipline can make or break you." I say that good discipline from the word of God can both break and make you. It can break you free from debilitating habits and sins and, from glory to glory, it can make you into a well-trained, well-disciplined, and wise child of God. In other words, it can truly make you free.

Heavenly Father, I know that you chasten me because you love me. Help me to welcome open rebuke rather than secret love. Train me and teach me. Drive every evil thought, speech, and action far from me. Lord, please make me and mold me each day into your image. I welcome your belt of truth. Amen

My Turn is Coming

"But as it is written, Eye hath not seen, nor ear heard, neither have entered into the heart of man, the things which God hath prepared for them that love him." I Corinthians 2:9

The Bible says to mourn with those who mourn and to rejoice with those who rejoice. It seems easier to have sympathy for people who are going through trials and tribulation. We will lift them up before the Lord in prayer. We will make sure everyone we know including the church puts the person on their prayer lists. We are there if they need a shoulder to cry on. However, when people we know announce they have just inherited a great deal of money, they received a huge promotion at work, they just lost over 50 pounds within six weeks, they just had a nose job and complete makeover and look 20 years younger, they just bought a nice home with little or no money down, they are taking a cruise to the Fuji Islands for three weeks, their book is a number one best seller, or they flash the new engagement ring they just received from a successful man, we smile and exclaim with as much excitement as we can squeeze through the uncontrollable pangs within the pit of our stomachs. We tell them how excited we are for them and wish them the best. We *are* happy for them; however, there is some selfish plea that emerges either in thought or word when we're alone that says, "Lord, why not me?"

No one, especially those of us who are saved, ever admit to feeling envious of others. It is one of those sins that are easy to hide. However, the Bible condemns it no less than any other type of sin. Did you find yourself in the list above? I did. It's easy to be happy for others when their good fortune is something you already have. However, it's not so easy when they seem to acquire something easily and more quickly than something for what you've been seeking, praying, and asking God for the last 10 years and still haven't received it. There was a time in my life when it seemed everyone around me, sisters with whom I'd prayed and cried with, were getting married. However, five years passed, then 10, then 15, and 20 years, and they all got married; everyone it seemed, except me. I had a friend who seemed to me that her spiritual life was suspect. She still used foul language from time to time. She married a minister who later became an elder in the church. I cried and cried to the Lord, but my cries were out of selfish desires. I see people who seem to have been borne with silver spoons in their mouths, while I suffer with continual debt and student loans I cannot afford to pay. To make matters worse, these people are not philanthropic as I am; neither do they have skills and abilities like I have to create employment and opportunities for others and to help the needy and poor. No matter how well meaning my motives may have appeared, I was still guilty of the two green-eyed sinful twins: jealousy and envy.

Jealousy occurs when you are resentful against the rivalry, success, or advantage of someone. It usually stems from fear that someone will take what you already have. Envy is the feeling of discontent and covetousness you feel because of the person's rivalry, success, or advantage. Fear, resentment, discontent, and then covetousness – they are psychologically and emotionally damaging to the soul. Jealousy and envy are the symptoms; covetousness is the resulting sin that the Bible addresses. (Exodus 20:17) All of the problems, fear, resentment, and discontentment take root within us when we stop trusting God. Perfect love dispels the fear. God says he will provide everything we need. (Philippians 4:19) When we fear losing someone we love, whether those fears are founded or not, we must remember that, despite what it appears, God has everything under control. Does it seem as though some man or woman is attracting the attention of your spouse? Does the man seem more handsome and successful, the woman prettier and more successful? One thing to remember is that affection is like a bird. If you hold it too tightly you'll crush it and it will die. But if you allow it to rest peacefully in the open palm of your hand and gently stroke its brow, there is a chance that it may fly away. If this happens, it was never yours to begin with. Ah, but if it comes back, it will belong to your forever.

Paul encourages us to be content with whatever we have and in whatever state we find ourselves. (Hebrews 13:5; Philippians 4:12) There is a saying that the grass is always greener on the other side, but it still has to be mowed. Sometimes we can jump from the frying pan right into the fire. It is best to trust and wait on God in every circumstance. Sometimes what we ask God for will not profit us, even though we may disagree. God knows what we all need and when. We should never measure ourselves with others, especially with gifts they receive. (2 Corinthians 10:12) Their successes and their advantages are theirs, but so is the responsibility that comes along with them. When people are blessed, believe it or not they need just as much prayer and ready-shoulders as those who mourn. Nothing bad lasts forever and nothing good lasts forever. Things and situations will change, especially for those of us who are saved. The Devil will never let up. So, when others rejoice, truly rejoice with them, but go home and say a prayer for them also. Thank God for his blessings, pray that they will be good stewards of what God has given them, and pray that God will bless them with more. Then remember that God is no respecter of persons. He will, in his own time, give you exactly what you need and desire. He promises this in his word, and "he is not a man that he should lie" (Numbers 23:19). Then, before you know it, it will soon be time for others to rejoice with you and lift you up in prayer.

> *Forgive me, Lord, I have been guilty of jealousy and envy. I have allowed fear, resentment, and discontent to reign in me. I have been guilty of coveting things that belong to others. I repent of it all. Help me to trust and wait on you. Help me to be content with such things as I have and to be thankful for your many blessings. Amen*

Timing is Everything

"I must work the works of him that sent me, while it is day: the night cometh, when no man can work." John 9:4

In the Book of Ecclesiastes, verses 3 through 9, we are told that to everything there is a season and there is time to every purpose under heaven. There is a time to be born and a time to die, a time to plant and a time to pluck up that which is planted, a time to kill and a time to heal, a time to laugh and a time to weep, a time to mourn and a time to dance, a time to cast away stones and a time to gather stones together, a time to embrace and a time to refrain from embracing, a time to get and a time to lose, a time to keep and a time to throw away, a time to rend and a time to sew, a time to keep silent and a time to speak, a time to love and a time to hate, and a time for war and a time for peace. These wise words came from a wise man, King Solomon.

Everything is perfect when it is in God's timing. We can cry, rant, and rave, but we cannot stop God's timing in anything. When we line up with God we'll know when our season and timing is. God created this world, the stars, the sun, the moon, and the planets: all created for a purpose. He separated the waters and created the dry land with all of its trees, mountains, and vegetation all for a specific purpose. He called it good. He instilled within everything he created a set of planetary and terrestrial laws to sustain their existence. He created animals and then he created mankind. God expertly created a world with everything he knew we would need to sustain our existence. However, in his infinite wisdom, he also made it temporal. His end goal is to eventually create a place for us to reign eternally. However, one question has to be answered first: Can we be trusted with eternity?

Heaven had already experienced turmoil due to Lucifer's rebellion. He, along with a third of the angels, now called demons, was ejected out of God's holy presence. Because

Lucifer continues to accuse and blame God, calling the Lord Almighty unjust, cruel, and tyrannical, this whole controversy must be played out to allow the other two-thirds of the angelic hosts to witness and see how treacherous a liar Lucifer, now called the Devil, truly is. All of Heaven must see that God is true, loving, gracious, and merciful; however, he is full of justice and rules with an omnipotent, powerful, and mighty hand. Lucifer, nor the fallen angels, has a chance for salvation. The pit of Hell was made and designed for them; however, Satan is content on taking as many prisoners as he can with him. (Matthew 25:41; Revelation 12:9) God proved his graciousness and mercy by sending his only Son to redeem us after Satan influenced us to fall. Man has a choice, a free-will, that is, a decision to choose life or choose death. Of course, Satan pulls out all stops to make sure man chooses the latter through sin.

I was born over 50 years ago. I hear people make claims that they were either born too late or born too soon. What they mean is they feel they should have been born during the era with which they seem to be more compatible or more comfortable. There are some young people born today who love the music of the 50's. There are people born in the 40's who created music so far ahead of their own time. Nobody understood them or appreciated them. Some say they were "a step out of time." Then there are people like me who they called "Preemies." Preemies are usually said to have been born premature, that is sooner than what the doctor predicted based on when the mother reported her first missed menstrual cycle. I was born during the 8th month of my mother's pregnancy instead of the 9th month. Yet who is to say I was born too soon? God, and God alone, knows the right timing. Since he knows the right timing of our birth, surely he knows the right timing of our death. There are so many people who do not live to see the age of 70. The age of 70 ("threescore years and ten) is what the Bible says is promised to man, that is, a reasonable or average life span. (Psalm 90:10) However, there were people like Adam and Eve, Noah, and Moses who lived for 800 or 900 years. However, even 900 years is still nothing compared to eternity.

It matters not how *long* we live in these temporal bodies. It does matter, however, *how* we live in these temporal bodies. God has promised that if we endure to the end, we will receive a crown of glory. We will receive new spiritual bodies and live in a new heaven and new earth prepared just for us. (Isaiah 65:17; Isaiah 66:22; 2 Peter 3:13; Revelation 21:1) Therefore, it is expedient for us to submit to God's omniscient and loving timing. Jesus (Yahoshua) is soon to return. No man knows the exact day or the hour, but we can be sure of his return. (Matthew 24:36) The signs are here. Look up, it's time and our "redemption draweth nigh." (Luke 21:28)

God, Alpha and Omega, I know you are perfect in all you do. I know your ways are not always my ways, and I know your timing is not always my timing. Help me to accept your timing. Help me to line up with your will and your way. Most of all, help me to be ready when you call me home. Amen

Armed with Courage

"Brethren, I count not myself to have apprehended: but this one thing I do, forgetting those things which are behind, and reaching forth unto those things which are before, I press toward the mark for the prize of the high calling of God in Christ Jesus." Philippians 3:13-14

I remember an old church song my grandmother used to sing:

> *"We are soldiers in the army*
> *We have to fight although we have die*
> *We have to hold up the bloodstained banner*
> *We have to hold it up until we die."*

The people who sang these songs knew that if you don't stand up for something, you'll fall for anything. In these short verses these people tell us who they are in Christ, what their purpose is, and what they intend to do. They know we are in a spiritual battle and that we are soldiers in God's army. One thing is also clear: they know they may have to pay the ultimate price of salvation with their lives.

Today, Christians in other countries are being slaughtered all day long. (Psalm 44:22; Romans 8:36) Most of us have yet to experience this type of persecution here in America; however, it is coming. (Matthew 24:9) Most of us are afraid to open our mouths to proclaim the goodness of Christ. Most of us are afraid to be the voice of reason and justice when we are the only ones who would be doing so. It's easy to have your voices blend in with the crowds and not be singled out. People like Amos, Daniel, Jeremiah, Isaiah, Deborah, Esther, and John the Baptist were not afraid to be the "voice of one crying in the wilderness."

Courage is rare and precious. People like Joan of Arc burned at the stake for fulfilling her call to fight for God. Dr. Martin Luther King fought against racial injustice and was allowed to go to the mountaintop but, like Moses, not allowed to cross over. Women like Sojourner Truth and Harriet Tubman risked their lives for a cause that was greater than the sum of their existence. John F. Kennedy and Abraham Lincoln were shot and killed for having the courage to take action against injustice. Brave young people, like Los Niños Héroes, valiantly gave their lives in the Mexican-American War. They had the courage to stand up for what was just and right, despite the consequences they knew they would suffer. Jesus and all of the apostles suffered death on the cross or death by the hand of angry mobs. Those named above are but a small representation of faithful soldiers. There are so many nameless and faceless courageous people of God who refused to stand by and do nothing. They, through faith in God, chose to sacrifice their lives for what was right. They chose to act.

There is a saying I've heard many times and have seen written down: "God grant me the courage to change the things I can change, the serenity to accept the things I cannot change, and the wisdom to know the difference." It is only through prayer and seeking God's will that we know what we can change and what we cannot. Sometimes we are the light bearers. We merely shine the light so others can see clear to continue the battle. Most of the time, we are the ones who pick up the sword of a slain soldier and continue the fight. Yes, we too will get slain, but there will be another who will pick up our sword and continue on. When we accepted Christ as our Savior, we were automatically enlisted into God's army. We received our orders (the Bible), we were trained by our leader (Jesus), and we are led into battle by our general (the Holy Ghost). We were given armor to protect us and heavy artillery (Word of God) to bring every thought and intent of the heart into subjection to Christ. (2 Corinthians 10:5) However, what good is our armor if we refuse to put it on daily. The Bible tells us to put on our armor because we wrestle not against flesh and blood but against principalities and powers and spiritual wickedness in high places. We have the belt of truth to support and hold us up and to hold up the rest of the armor. We have the shoes already directed to lead us where we need to go to preach the gospel. We have the breastplate of the righteousness of Christ. We have the helmet of salvation to remind us who we are: redeemed sinners who have been saved by grace. We have the shield of faith to deflect all satanic darts of doubt, depression, or discouragement. We have the Sword of the Spirit, that powerfully two-edged sword that is quick and powerful, able to divide asunder joint and marrow and discern every thought and intent of the heart. (Ephesians 6:10-17; Hebrews 4:12) We have the protection and artillery. However, without the God-instilled courage to go along with it, we are like cowardly lions roaring loudly until someone refuses to back down.

God is angry with sinners every day. (Psalm 7:11) He hates injustice and oppression. We, who are made in his image, can we be no less? Can we sit by and close our ears to the cries of those who are hurting? Can we shut our eyes and allow scales to accumulate on them because we refuse to see sin in its true light? Can we silence our voices and refuse to speak up when we know in fact that "the emperor" is wearing "no clothes?" Christ promised that he would be with us and that he would never leave us nor forsake us. (Hebrews 13:5) We are then without excuses. Our cowardice will find us out. One thing of which we can be sure is that God will hold us accountable because inaction is also a choice.

> *My God, he who is omnipotent, omniscient, and omnipresent, forgive me for my Laodicean state. Forgive me for my lack of faithfulness and inaction. Help me to recognize and know what I must do to continue this spiritual battle. Help me to know when I must speak and when I must act. Give me the words that I must speak. May I have the courage to stand up and fight even though it may mean my earthly life. Amen*

Avoiding the Extreme Makeover

"All things are lawful for me, but all things are not expedient: all things are lawful for me, but all things edify not."
I Corinthians 10:23

Ever meet a Type "A" personality? They seem to do everything to the "Nth Degree." They are never just cold; they are freezing. They are never just sick; they are dying. They are never just hungry; they are starving. They never just like someone; they are madly in love. Usually, they are the ones who become compulsive gamblers and over-eaters. In a word, they are extremists. Although this quality to go beyond the limits can be a liability for them and for others, when channeled in the right way, this quality can also be valuable. They are also the over-achievers who never settle for less. They are the ones who become managers and leaders who make the organization successful. They appreciate time and usually arrive early. When they are wrong they are all the way wrong. When they are right they are all the way right. There is no middle of the road. No one can ever accuse them of being "lukewarm."

Doesn't this over-achiever syndrome sound a lot like Saul who later became the apostle Paul? He persecuted the church due to his zeal and belief that the Sanhedrin was absolutely right. (Philippians 3:5-6; Acts 26:14) Paul was convinced beyond a shadow of a doubt that the Hebrews following Jesus and this new "sect" were blasphemous and worthy of death. He believed this with all of his heart. This should teach us that just because someone is sincere, does not mean they are right in their sincerity. However, these same individuals, these extremists, Type A personalities, are the same ones, who, when converted, are the very movers and shakers God wants to use for his service. We know this to be true because once Saul was "knocked off his high horse," he became Paul, a mighty preacher, teacher, and evangelist for the gospel of Christ. Not many others proved as faithful and dedicated as he who once persecuted the church.

So, where does temperance come into play? How do we distinguish it from lack of diligence, complacency, and the state of being "lukewarm?" Temperance means self-restraint, self-control, or moderation, especially with regard to indulgence in appetite or desires. Temperance is also one of the gifts of the Spirit that Paul noted in Galatians, Chapter 5. In other words, we should avoid excess in our indulgence of self-directed pleasures. The Bible does not say that a healthy appetite is wrong, but it does warn against over-doing it. However, this over-indulgence and lack of temperance can manifest itself in other ways.

I remember when I was a member of the Seventh-Day Adventist Church I read and was taught a great deal about natural health and healing. I even read the *Ministry of Healing* by Ellen White. My children were young and I was convinced we should become vegetarians. I believe they are fashionably called "Veggies," today. However, we were vegetarians that ate eggs and cheese. Some vegetarians will not only abstain from eating animal flesh, they also forego eating the products that animals produce. Being the Type "A" personality that I am, I would not allow my children to eat anything with sugar, caffeine, or any other man-made ingredients that I knew were potentially harmful for the body. This went on for two years until I got to a point one day where I felt I could "kill" for a hamburger.

That experience reminded me of those growing up in the "holiness" or Pentecostal churches. They were not allowed to go to parties, go swimming, or play sports. They could go to church six or seven days a week, do chores, and go to school. This made for a pretty boring childhood and puberty for many, who, later in life, ran amuck because they had been denied these pleasures. Some of them became extremists in harmful pleasures because of this. The leaders in these churches did what they thought was right. However, the Bible teaches us to practice temperance in all things. You can go overboard in either direction. Most people, if you ask them, will say the Bible says you should not drink wine. However, the Bible says not to be drunk with wine. (Ephesians 5:18) There is a difference. This is why the Sadducees and Pharisees accused Jesus and his disciples of being wine-bibbers. (Luke 7:33-34) Some will even tell you that the Bible says having money is wrong, but the Bible says it is the "love of money" that becomes a snare and should be avoided. (I Timothy 6:10) The Sadducees and Pharisees had even bogged down the 4th Commandment, that says to keep the Sabbath day holy, with so many man-made "do's" and "don'ts," that it lost its true purpose of what God intended and made the day a burden to many instead of a restful holy day to commune with God and fellow man. (Mark 7:13) It seems the best rule of thumb is to be led by prayer and the word of God. And, we should remember that temperance, that is, self-restraint and self-control, refers to oneself, not necessarily the requirements we want to put on others. (Romans 14:1-23)

Yahweh, forgive my overzealous nature whereby I find myself out on a limb and eventually out of your will. I want to exercise Godly self-control to serve you in Spirit and in truth. If I must go overboard, let it be in loving others so much that I help pull them out of the fires of Hell by witnessing to them about repentance of sins and the good news of salvation. Amen

Going for the Gold or God

"Look not every man on his own things, but every man also
on the things of others." Philippians 2:4

We live in a world today where the athletic mentality of being the best and beating the other guy is the "name of the game." I am amazed at how fanatical people become with their favorite professional or college ball teams. They paint their faces, their clothes, and their bodies with words and signs to stand out and let everyone known for whom they are rooting. I've watched them get into shouting matches with referees and rival team supporters over a decision they believed to be wrong. I've been grieved to hear how lives were lost and people injured because of a night of celebration after a big win where they just had to get drunk, turn over cars, and beat up everybody. I am also bewildered when I learn that coaches are fired and players are traded because the team didn't win. However, after a win the coaches are lauded, the players making the most points are congratulated and sometimes given a "Most Valuable Player" trophy, but everyone will espouse how it was really the "team effort" that resulted in their success.

I hear talk about "win-win" situations; however, only rarely, without any memory jogs, does anyone remember who took the Silver or the Bronze Olympic medal, but they almost always remember who brought home the Gold. Whenever there is competition, someone wins and someone loses. There is no other way around it. When people play for "fun" as they call it, this means the usual tangible stakes are not in jeopardy. However, self-esteem and egos is usually the intangible stakes that people feel they cannot afford to lose. This mentality pervades the employment field in the form of office politics. You see it in the social arena, the education arena, and especially politics. With this type of mentality, eventually we all lose. It is because of the pride, ego, and selfish desires within our hearts that lead us to compete to the point where the other person is left destitute, torn down, and we end up with all of their "chips."

We watch as the person limps away with nothing and in our smugness we retort, "Well, they shouldn't have been playing if they couldn't afford to lose." This same attitude and hard-heartedness is why capitalism does not work in our society. Many are left with nothing because of those who want, no – who *must* have everything. True healthy competition results when each player strives to be the best that he or she can be. You do your absolute best. When you lose you know you did everything you could and you congratulate your temporary opponent and wish them well. When you win you congratulate your temporary opponent and wish them well.

However, the most dangerous arena is in the church. I've witnessed sisters and brothers get into verbal altercations that almost result in physical blows. I've heard about church meetings where brothers ended up physically attacking each other. I've seen long-time friendships end over the love and affection of a sister or brother who ended up with neither of the competitors. I've seen preachers and ministers obviously try to out-preach another speaker. I've seen choir members try to out-sing the lead singer. In addition to the "solo" competition, I've seen many of them cluster into unofficial "cliques" to out-do the other so-called non-existent (so they say) "cliques" in the church. Even the disciple brothers, James and John, requested that Jesus allow them to sit on the right and left of Jesus in Heaven. Their goal was to be at the head of the other disciples. They wanted the "choice seats" in the house. The other 10 disciples became angry when they heard that James and John had made this request, even though Jesus said it was not his to give but to whom God had already prepared. Jesus corrected their understanding and even reproved them for their selfishness. Jesus told them that he who is the greatest is the servant, so unlike what the world teaches us. (Matthew 20:20-28) We are taught to be number one at all costs. However, the Bible tells we are unwise to compare ourselves with ourselves. (2 Corinthians 10:12) We are one in Christ Jesus. It was Jesus who let us understand that being the greatest is not as Muhammad Ali had claimed who said we should, "float like a butterfly and sting like a bee." According to Jesus, being the greatest means, "exalting others while humbling me."

> *Lord, forgive me for desiring to be better than everybody else at all costs. Weed out the prideful ego that leads me to compete and spar with my fellow man. Help me to exalt you above others. Help me to exalt others above myself. Help me to minister and to serve and do all that I do to your wonderful glory and not mine. Amen*

The Right Path of Worship

"I am the Lord your God who took you out of the land of Egypt, out of the prison-house of bondage. You are to have no other gods but me."
Exodus 20:2-3

The Bible is clear in its position regarding idolatry. Exodus 20:4-5 warns against making any graven (carved or sculptured) image of anything in heaven or in the earth, and instructs us not to bow down and worship them. I think this it is interesting that the Catholic Church removed this commandment and split up one of the other commandments to make sure there were still ten. This is a perfect example of disobeying the first commandment by taking the word and creating your own type of god to suit your own purposes. In fact, since they removed and revised the second commandment, the Catholic Church feels they can now bow down and worship graven images of those whom they have made "saints" such as Mary, the mother of Jesus, Peter, Paul, and John, to name a few. They also confess their sins to a man on earth, the Pope. Jesus said no man on earth has authority to forgive sins except he who is God. In other words, they have made the Pope equal to God, which is idolatry in the highest form.

Most of us can recognize this type of idolatry. We even understand that we can make idols of money, cars, homes, and even loved ones and self. Idolatry is actually "excessive or blind adoration, reverence, or devotion to anything or anyone" other than Yahweh. People lie, rob, and kill to acquire their idols, to keep their idols, and to protect them. It is hard to watch the news because it is filled with reports of crimes committed by individuals on behalf of and for their idols. One of the most disturbing types of idolatry is that of celebrities. This is why reality shows are so popular. Anyone appearing on TV is an instant celebrity, no matter who they are. It seems people don't care if the person is moral, immoral, or amoral. The word "fan" is just a short form of the word "fanatic" which is a person who has an "extreme uncritical enthusiasm and zeal." This extreme, uncritical enthusiasm or zeal can be religious, political, or otherwise. However, today most people have tempered the meaning and use it as a complimentary term with respect to celebrities and professional athletes. The most satanic is Lady Gaga who refers to her fans as "Little Monsters."

One fatal example of this extreme, uncritical enthusiasm and zeal is seen in the Jim Jones massacre that took place in Jonestown, Africa in 1978. It is heart-breaking that of the 1,000 members, only 33 survived the suicide-murder pact designed and led by the deranged Rev. Jim Jones. These people blindly followed a man who tried to create a socialist paradise. Some of them had come to their senses and tried to escape what they saw in reality as a slave camp. The evidence of sin and words spoken contrary to the Word of God are red flags that should warn every believer that they have enlisted into the wrong camp. They should run away as fast as Joseph did from Potiphar's wife who tried to ensnare him into adultery with her. For some reason people want to remember the few days when everything was going well. They would rather focus on the few times when the leader was kind to them, preached the house down, and made them feel like they belonged. They forget that the Devil can appear as an angel of light and that he is a devious and treacherous liar with war in his heart though his words may be "smooth as butter" (Psalm 55:21). He lays a trap for your very soul.

One type of idolatry that most people, especially those who consider themselves to be a "good person," is when they find their consciences convicting them of violating the law of God and therefore, find themselves out of God's will, and they attempt to create their own god. Some of them will say that God is too loving and too kind to send anyone to Hell. I've heard others say, "God would not judge me; he would let me go free and send me to Heaven because he understands that I'm only human." Of course their god would act in this way — because he doesn't exist. They are guilty of idolatry because they have created their own type of god. Their god will not send them to Hell for sin and let them into Heaven. They try to bypass acknowledgement of their personal sinful state whereby they need a savior. Their hearts are not converted, they are not repentant, and most likely they plan to keep on sinning.

God is a God of love but he is also a God of judgment. Yahweh is his name. His law is like his immutable nature; it does not change to fit our purposes and state of mind and action. (Malachi 3:6) There is nothing more important than our eternal salvation. If we are to escape with our spiritual garments intact, it behooves us to quench the fires of idolatry in our lives. Even the smoldering embers that initially appear harmless and non-threatening should be stomped out immediately. We are called to "lay aside every weight and the sin that so easily besets us" so that we can "run with patience the race that is set before us" (Hebrews 12:1).

Yahweh, the one and only true and merciful God, forgive my foolishness and blind allegiance to things and to mankind. I place everything I own, everything I have, and everything I am at your feet. It all belongs to you; I am just the steward. Lead me into your paths everlasting. You are forever the only captain of my faith. Amen

The Color of Lies

"But the fearful, and unbelieving, and the abominable, and murderers, and whoremongers, and sorcerers, and idolaters, and all liars, shall have their part in the lake which burneth with fire and brimstone: which is the second death." Revelation 21:8

I attended a conference the other day where the facilitator gave an example of bending the rules by telling a short anecdote from her own life whereby she bent the rules and acted contrary to policy. She said that when one of her tall surly-looking co-workers ("the enforcer") asked if she was the one who had committed the deed, she asked him why. After he retorted that the person who had committed the deed would have "hell to pay," she quickly responded, "It wasn't me." She then commented to us, "I'm a Catholic, so I can lie and then go to confession." Though we find this amusing, sadly, it is also true.

It's amazing how we categorize our sins. Most of us are not guilty of the big, awful, and "unforgivable" sins such as murder, rape, bank robbery, and manslaughter due to drunk driving. Neither are we guilty of the medium, moderate, and "white-collar" sins such as embezzlement, tax fraud, and minor assault. We, on occasion, may be guilty of the little, insignificant, and "everybody does it" sins such as borrowing without asking, gossip, and lying. Of course by "lying," we always mean "little white lies." Interesting how society puts the word "white" at the beginning of a sin and suddenly it is no longer viewed as something terrible. The bad news is God sees sin as sin and he is no respecter of color.

My mother used to warn us never to lie to her. She said that if a person lied then they would probably steal. She said she hated liars and thieves. She then told us that if we lied and she found out it would be worse than if we had told the truth. Yes, we would still get punished either way, but the punishment would be far worse if we lied. So, I grew up with this mentality. My son and my ex-husband were two of the most compulsive liars I had ever encountered. I used to drive both of them crazy because they couldn't understand how I always discovered the truth. I told my son that since he was my child, I knew everything about him. I also told him that whatever I didn't know instinctually or discover for myself, God would tell me. This is exactly what would happen. Once discovered in a lie, my son would respond that he "had to lie." He is now over 30 years old and a sergeant in the military and I'd like to think his mindset has changed.

Unfortunately, at the time, my son, like a great number of people, actually believed he had to lie. For some reason, it is viewed as self-preservation. When people are threatened the old "fight or flight" syndrome kicks in. Lying is the preferred and chosen escape route. In fact, this road is so dangerous that the liar finds himself or herself creating more and more escape routes. One of the problems is the escape routes eventually lead to a dead end (Hell).

Hey, wait a minute, didn't the people in the Bible tell lies? Yes, they did, all the time. Abraham told a half-truth when he told the Pharaoh in Egypt, who was enamored with Sarah, that Sarah was his sister. Abraham feared the Pharaoh would kill him and everyone else, so he lied. Sarah was his half-sister but she was also his wife. (Genesis 12:11-20; 20:1-12). Like father, like son, Isaac did the same thing with his wife, Rebecca. (Genesis 26:7). However, a half-truth is the same as half-Strychnine – it's still a killer poison. Rahab, the harlot, lied and saved the lives of the spies sent by Joshua. She hid the spies, and when asked where the spies were, she responded, "They went that way" and pointed in the wrong direction. Because Abraham and Isaac were blessed of God, because Rahab is inducted into the "hall of faith" along with Abraham in Hebrews, chapter 11, many believe God condoned this type of lying. Some point to scriptures and try to justify this view by saying that God approves of certain types of lying while detesting other types of lying. Because God does not automatically strike dead everyone who lies or who has lied in the Bible, even though Ananias and Sapphira (husband and wife) were struck dead because they lied to the Holy Ghost, well-meaning teachers believe God condones some types of lying while he excuses other types. This, in and of itself, is blasphemy. God does not distinguish one lie from another; however, man does. People in the Bible also committed adultery, murdered, raped, stole, coveted, committed idolatry, defiled the Sabbath, dishonored parents, and blasphemed the name of God. In some cases people lost their lives; other times they did not. In some cases, God took their lives; other times he did not. Yes, Abraham, Isaac and Rahab lied. They also committed other sins, but they also committed acts of faith. David broke almost all of the commandments, but he was the "Lone Ranger" in standing up for God against Goliath and the Philistines and is considered a man after God's own heart (1 Samuel 13:14; Acts 13:22).

God is angry with sin every day, yet he wants no one to perish. He is giving sinners time to repent and to turn to him. Many of the prophets, including Moses, disobeyed God, yet he did not destroy them. He does not "throw out the baby with the bath water." God hates lying as he does all sins. It, along with any sin of which is not confessed and repented, will result in the fires of Hell. At one time the children of Israel were required to sacrifice an animal such as a lamb or a goat; however, since Jesus was the last lamb who was slain for our sins, we need only confess, repent, ask for forgiveness, and turn to him for salvation and not to man. We don't keep sinning (lying) because we feel we can just "go to confession." However, when we do fall we know that we have an advocate with the father. He says that if we "confess our sins he is faithful and just to forgive us our sins and cleanse us from all unrighteousness" (1 John 1:9).

> *Father, I know that you hate a lying tongue. Forgive me for half-truths and for making excuses. I repent of all deception. Cast away from me this evil spirit. Give me the courage to speak truth and to know when to remain silent. Thank you for your grace and mercy. Amen*

Fit as a Fiddle

"What? know ye not that your body is the temple of the Holy Ghost which is in you, which ye have of God, and ye are not your own?"
I Corinthians 6:19

As I celebrate my 54th birthday today, I take time to reflect on the "shape" I'm in, or rather lack thereof. Though I'm not sickly as most people, I'm still not the healthiest. The last doctor's visit was about three years ago. The nurse couldn't understand why I weighed so much, but I knew. All of my blood work and tests were fine except I had high blood pressure. The doctor wanted to prescribe pills. I protested and he began to warn me that I could have a stroke. I hadn't taken any medication for over 10 years at that time. I'd learned not to argue with him so I took the prescription and threw it away when I got home. The visit to the gynecologist was pretty much the same. The doctor told me I should get on some of the "wonderful pills" like the ones she was taking for her blood pressure. The look on her face reminded me of a crazed drug addict. I treated my blood pressure with Vitamin C, Hawthorne Berries, Garlic, and other natural blood pressure relieving herbs. The nurse called me a week later and said the doctor wanted to see me the following week for a follow-up visit. I made the appointment and saw him the next week. When he took my blood pressure, he had a huge smile on his face and said, "Those pills are working." My only comment was, "Really?"

It seems as though cysts and tumors run in our family. My visit to the chiropractor three years ago also revealed, from the x-ray, that my body is loaded with them. I'll never forget the look on the chiropractor's face. He is a Christian man and I could see the sympathy in his face. I could tell he was wondering how I was walking around alive. He barely touched me when I asked for an adjustment. I think he believed I would break. I've known for a long time I have cancer in my body; most of us do. Usually, the cells just lie dormant until some drug or unnatural chemical triggers it. Most people would never believe it to look at me but I weighed myself and I was almost 180 pounds. I'm

5'4". A great deal of the weight is due to the tumors in my body. Even so, I know that I need to go back on the macrobiotic diet, not only for health reasons but to lose about 20-30 pounds. I did this many years ago when a doctor wanted to schedule me for surgery when he discovered I had tumors. I would not allow him to do so. He ranted and raved about him not being responsible if something happened to me, so I put his fears to rest by signing a waiver of liability.

I realize that I'm still alive because of God's grace and mercy, and because I don't take any medication, not even aspirin for a headache or cold medicine when I get a cold or the flu, which is rare. God created the human body that the Bible calls the holy temple and everything in the earth, air, and water to sustain our lives. (I Corinthians 3:17; I Corinthians 6:19) Anything man-made and chemically manufactured like drugs and medications is contrary to our systems. Yes, some of these drugs will ease our pain and even seem to eliminate the problem; however, we find later that the drug has caused some other problem and the doctor promptly prescribes another drug for this new ailment. So, on and on it goes. Is it any wonder that the President's first order of business was to enact a mandated healthcare bill so that doctors and especially pharmaceutical companies can continue to make billions and billions of dollars? There is a natural herb and remedy for every human ailment. Every fatal disease can be prevented, and if contracted, can be cured. Scientists and pharmaceutical companies know this. But where is the financial profit if everyone is cured? Also, they would lose billions they now receive for "research" to create yet one more drug. It is the goal of pharmaceutical companies that men, women, and children are on some type of drug from the moment they are born until the day they die. They have almost accomplished this goal.

We can only do so much today to keep healthy. Our water, air, and food are being poisoned with chemicals and drugs. Even so, we should abstain from habits such as smoking and eating and drinking processed items containing too much sugar, sugar substitutes, caffeine, and white starch. Our diets need to be low acidic and high alkaline. There is a saying that you are what you eat. If we want to live we should eat foods that are alive like natural vegetables and fruits, nuts and grains, and drink water – lots of the purest water you can find. The intake amount should be half our body weight in ounces. Yes, you will make frequent urination visits but you'll feel better and be much healthier. We should rid ourselves of the aversion to pain so much that we opt for every prescription or over-the-counter drug that is recommended. None of this is sin that will keep us out of heaven, but it will make for a better temporal existence and maybe even prolong our lives. I've heard some people quip, "Why die healthy?" as an excuse for not taking care of themselves. However, our bodies were created for God's purpose. He cares just as much for our physical well-being as he does for our spiritual well-being. We are his instruments. We owe it to him to keep ourselves as finely tuned as possible. Imagine the great symphony of witnesses we can be!

Lord, I know that my body is your holy temple and that you created me in your image. Forgive me when I defile your temple in any respect. Help me to take care of everything you have entrusted me, including this holy temple. When I am ill, may prayer and both your natural and spiritual provision heal and sustain me. Amen

Taking Out the Garbage

*"But I say unto you, that every idle word that men shall speak, they shall
give account thereof in the day of judgment."*
Matthew 12:36

We are natural born communicators. We send out
messages, expect and receive feedback and responses, translate
these messages, and then repeat the process over again. Word
of mouth is by far the fastest mode of communication; however,
it is also the most unreliable. There are cultures who
communicate solely through word of mouth. Even generations
and histories are retold this way. Many years passed by before
the Bible was actually written down. However, the Bible is
reliable because we know that "holy men of God spake as they
were moved by the Holy Ghost (2 Peter 1:21). It is the inspired
word of God. There are no contradictions; however, Bible
writers focused on specific details from their own perspectives.
Nonetheless, the harmonious and central message is ever
present. These writers, as do all communicators, had an
unselfish motive for relaying information, especially information
about the life of Christ. What about our motives when relaying
information about the lives of others?

How many times have we either told others, either in
person or via phone, to please pray for a brother or sister in
Christ and then began to report all of the sins or problems with
which the individual is being plagued or committing? Do we
really need to make the requested intercessor aware of exactly
what's going on? Some will say that prayers need to be specific,
so we must let them know why they are praying. However, we
also have to ask ourselves whether or not the request for
prayer for these individuals is not just an excuse to gossip about
their lives and the problems going on. Gossip is characterized as
"idle talk or rumor" especially with regard to the personal and
private lives of others. The difference between news and gossip
is whether or not the report is factual, whether or not we were
first-hand witnesses, the significance of the event, and especially
our motive for making the report. The Bible says that we will

106

have to give an account for every idle word spoken. Idle words are stagnant in purpose and use. They are not dynamic and full of life. They do not move anyone or anything forward. In other words, to engage in such is a waste of time. We will have to give an account to God for such a waste of time.

There is a saying, "Small people talk about other people, average people talk about material things, and great people talk about ideas." I am not a materialistic person, so when people engage in such banter I listen but this is as far as it goes. When people talk about making life better and improving situations, I get excited and am moved to action. However, when people discuss things going on with others, I still listen, but I am also left feeling burdened. I feel as though someone has taken a truck load of garbage and dumped it right in my lap. Of course I'm using this as a simile, but in the literal sense, if I knew someone was standing in front of me and did this, I would be upset and angry. So, why do we sit and watch silently while people bring in their trash can and sit it in front of us, then remove the top, pick up the can, and slowly pour out its contents? We should immediately stop them the moment we are aware they are bringing in this garbage. We should let them know that we maintain a clean house and do not wish to have it defiled with gossip. I know of only one person who did this many years ago when I attempted to make derogatory statements about someone. She immediately changed the subject. In other words, she would not allow me to dump the garbage I was carrying.

When we are first-hand witnesses to the faults and sins of others, the Bible tells us to pray for them and that love will cover these sins. (1 Peter 4:8) Notice the word does not say "to cover up" the sins. We pray for the erring one to confess and repent of these sins. We follow the Bible's method for dealing with such and must remember that the goal is reconciliation not condemnation. Yes, we do have a responsibility to help the erring brother or sister, but before we go to someone about God, we must first go to God about the person. Through prayer, God will give you wisdom as to what to say, how to say it, and when to say it. Our responsibility is to go to the person in love with a goal to reconcile them back to Christ. If the person will not hear you and continues to sin, we are to take another brother or sister with us. If the erring brother or sister still continues to sin, we are then to bring them before the church. If the person is still unrepentant and continues to sin, then and only then are we to have no more dealings with them. (Matthew 18:15-18); 1 Corinthians 5:9-13) This process moves the situation forward and moves others to action. Hopefully, it will move the erring one who has become defiled to clean up his or her act.

> *Father, forgive my tendency to listen to and engage in idle talk and rumors. Give me the courage to rebuke in love anyone who attempts to engage in gossip in my presence. Help me to work to restore my brother or sister who may be in sin or whose situation needs repair. May I consider myself and bring my tendencies into subjection lest I fall into the same temptation. Thank you for your grace and mercy. Amen*

Always Room for One More

"Let not your heart be troubled: have faith in God and have faith in me. In my Father's house are rooms enough; if it was not so, would I have said that I am going to make ready a place for you? And if I go and make ready a place for you, I will come back again and will take you to be with me, so that you may be where I am." John 14:1-3

As I get closer and closer to the end of my earthly existence, I am painfully aware that I still lack one crucial element in my life: a sexually intimate companion, that is, a husband. I've been divorced 26 years, almost as long as some people have been married. Throughout my ministry I've come into contact with many sisters in Christ with whom I've prayed that we would all receive husbands. Fortunately for them, not only would they receive husbands but they would end up marrying well. I praise God for this. However, it has not been the case with me. For a long time I brooded and cried and pleaded with God to explain to me why this was so. Mostly, God has been silent. I even wrote a book on the subject and called it, *Dear God, Why Am I Still Single?* Eventually, I republished it and called it *Why I Should Hate Men, But Don't.* Though I still don't have all of the answers, God has given me peace.

Statistics show that after the age of 35, women have a better chance of getting captured by terrorists than they do of getting married. I used to joke about how I couldn't even get captured by terrorists. I stopped doing this after 9-11. Further statistics show that the majority of black women head single households. I know this is not because they want it this way, but because many of our black men have abandoned us. We are today's unwanted commodity, not because there is something defective or wrong with us, but because of bad press and poor marketing. Satan's goal has been the extinction of the original people of God. We are that people, the Black Hebrews. Television, movies, every media is perfectly designed to separate black men from black women while at the same time exalting every other race of women. There are so many historical and culturally embedded roots of this problem that only God can heal our broken hearts.

Many black women have opted to date and/or marry white men who are usually much older than they are. Of course, these black women are successful in their own right and are what society would call good looking. Most women of other races, especially white women, do not have to be successful; they need only possess what society has deemed as "great beauty." It appears this quality is anything that is totally opposite from having dark skin, African facial features, and wooly hair. Satan has managed to fool everyone and makes them believe that having "less" makes them better. Every race of people came from the black race. We have more and are made to feel less than. Many white people know their origins and they know the truth. They have been trying to hide who they are for thousands of years, and have been successful. However, I know that many white people would be devastated if they knew the truth.

It is my honest belief that if I were a white woman my life would be totally different. Without question, with my talents, abilities, education, and what I've been able to accomplish, I would no doubt be a wealthy woman and married. However, I truly love my brown skin and being who I am: a person created in God's image. It's so difficult because everything in this world revolves around image. If you don't have the right image you won't prosper. A great commodity is nothing if no one knows about it and it is not packaged and marketed in such a way as to create a desire to possess it. For example, years ago thousands of people clamored over each other to be the first to purchase the Pet Rock, making its creator extremely wealthy, before they realized their stupidity. If someone is on television, they become an instant celebrity and people buy what they are selling. One case in point is the father and son who own a pawn shop in Las Vegas and who sell rare items. When they were televised, their sales increased tremendously. Mostly, however, this only happens for non-black individuals.

Most black males have become the objects of desire because they have made and still make millions of dollars running with a ball across a goal line, putting a ball into a hoop, hitting a ball into a little cup, and also playing, singing, and dancing. Black women have erroneously believed that these successful and wealthy black men run toward white women and every other race of women except black women. The truth is these women have run toward them first. However, it is black women who have been labeled "gold diggers" when this could be farther from the truth. If you ask most black women what they want in a husband, they will tell you they want someone to love them who will be faithful and will contribute financially to the household. Most black women don't ask for much, but they get even less than that. This contributes to loneliness.

Loneliness is characterized as the painful awareness of the lack of meaningful contact with others. The sense of belonging, the need to love and be loved, is a human need. God created us as social beings. We need: 1) to know that we are significant and important to others, 2) intimate love from the opposite sex, and 3) the highest love that only God can provide. Although it is not the ideal, we can live without the first two; however, when people feel that all three are lacking, especially because they are unsaved and therefore do not know the love of Christ, they feel an emptiness that nothing can fill. Some will try to fill this void with drugs, alcohol, food, material items, and illicit sex. However, because these things provide only temporary satisfaction, a great number of lonely individuals end up taking their own lives.

One of the reasons God tells us not to "forsake the assembling" of ourselves with each other is to avoid anyone feeling lonely. (Hebrews 10:25) We are to care for each other and take care of the needs of each other. Unfortunately, not all of us will live out our lives with a mate. Sometimes the grace of God must be sufficient for us. Feelings and emotions can be deceptive and should not be the gauge for a rewarding life. God's word is what we trust and on which we must stand. God promised that he would never leave us nor forsake us (Hebrews 13:5). No matter what race we are, no matter our social or financial status, no matter what we look like, Christ died for each and every one of us. When we feel lonely, let us stand on his word and his promises. We can come to him, our friend, and lay our burdens upon him for his "yoke is easy" and his "burden is light." (Matthew 11:28-30) We can allow the King of Glory to come in and he will dine with us. (Revelation 3:20). We are never alone.

Father, let not my feelings and emotions control me. I know that I belong to you. I know that you care about my every need. I know that I am never alone. Help me to remember that I have so many brothers and sisters in Christ who love me. May I remember to fellowship with them. May I also remember that no matter how much they love me, the love you provide is without equal and without end. Amen

Herein is Love

"Greater love hath no man than this, that a man lay down his life for his friends." John 15:13

I can only think of one friendship that I've maintained since the age of 9. We grew up in the same neighborhood; in fact, her house was just around the corner and within walking distance. We are the same age except she was the youngest in her family and I was the oldest. Even though my family moved away when I was in my 2nd year of high school and our lives took different paths, we've kept in touch and visit each other during some of the major events in our lives. When we can't visit, we call, email, and/or send greeting cards. She has been married for a long time, has no post-secondary degrees, works as a civil servant, owns property and manages to save her money, and has no biological children but is a stepmother of one son. I've been divorced for a long time, have several degrees, work as a teacher and writer, own nothing and never manage to save any money, and have two biological children. One thing I can say about my friend is that I know she always "has my back." We don't always agree on everything, and after we've made sure the other knows exactly where we stand on an issue, we know how to agree to disagree. There have been occasions when we have unintentionally offended each other. We let the other know that this has occurred; forgiveness is either expressed or implied, and we move on to the next part of our lives.

I have another friend who, for the past 28 years, has lived in New York while I lived in California and then Arizona. We have not physically seen each other for all of those years, yet we used to talk to each other so often you would think we lived around the corner from each other. Then there are friends with whom I don't get to either see very often or communicate, yet I know that if I need them, they will be there to help me as much as possible. These are friends with whom I can call and have prayer. Of course, family members can also be friends. However, I have family members who I would call friends and I have family members who I would not call friends. My daughter is probably my best friend.

All of these are friendships that most of us take for granted; however, many people have no such friends. There are some people who are work associates, acquaintances, and friends of convenience. Of course, there are "fair weather" friends: people who make a pretense of being a true friend when things are going well. However, when trouble ensues or there is the slightest chance their needs will not be met, they quickly become "wear feather" friends and fly away. It becomes apparent these people have been merely using you for their own selfish goals.

The Bible says there is a friend that sticks closer than a brother. David and Jonathan were two such friends. When Jonathan and David met they knew they would be brothers for life, despite the fact that Jonathan's father, Saul, repeatedly tried to kill David. Ruth and Naomi shared a fatal tragedy of a common loved one, yet they remained close to each other. This was a mentor relationship where Naomi, older and wiser, looked out for and taught Ruth, who was younger and more vulnerable. Of course, some friends, even though they stick closer than a brother, can and will betray us. Jesus chose 12 disciples, and unlike us, knew that one of them was a devil. (John 6:70) What is so amazing is that, with this knowledge, Jesus treated Judas no differently than the other disciples. In fact, he gave Judas great responsibility. He even called him friend. Jesus – while dying on the cross after enduring beatings, whippings, mocking, nails driven into his hands and feet, piercings from a crown of thorns on his head and a sword in his side, and the worst kind of betrayal and humiliation – prayed that God would forgive his enemies and his friends who forsook him. This he did with his last dying breath. (Luke 23:34)

We sing a song that says, *What a friend we have in Jesus.* There could be no better friend than him. No one has or will ever accomplish what he has for us. He is definitely a friend that has shown he is friendly, as the Bible tells us to do if we want to have friends. (Proverbs 18:24) Among other things, Jesus (Yahoshua) is our counselor, our mediator, our deliverer, our provider, and our comforter. He redeemed us from death and promises to never leave us nor forsake us. We know him as the one true friend, but friendship is mutual. Do we reciprocate his everlasting friendship or do we "crucify him afresh" by our disobedience? (Hebrews 6:6) Jesus said that if we love him we should obey him. He gave us two commandments on which hang all the law. First, our friend commanded us to love God, the Father, with all our hearts, minds, and soul. (Matthew 22:37-38) Second, he commanded us to love our neighbors as ourselves. (Matthew 22:39-40) In other words, in thought, word, and deed he wanted us to be a true friend to God and to man. In so doing, we establish both vertical (Godly and heavenly) and horizontal (man and earthly) relationships. Though man will often let us down and even betray us and though God will often judge us and not look upon us because of our sin, Christ is the bridge that represents both the vertical and horizontal that keeps us connected to both. It is he who heals and mends all broken fellowships and friendships.

My Lord and Savior, thank you for teaching me what true friendship really is. Forgive me when I fall short of your glory in this area. Help me to love unconditionally and to forgive continually. Thank you, most of all, for being my friend. Amen

Joy Comes After the Mourning

"In place of my food I have grief, and cries of sorrow come from me like water. For I have a fear and it comes on me, and my heart is greatly troubled. I have no peace, no quiet, and no rest; nothing but pain comes on me."
Job 3:24-26

What can you say to someone who has lost something or someone very dear to them? "Cheer up, things will get better?" "It's not that bad?" "You know, this reminds me of a time when . . .?" Usually, the best response is to let the grief-stricken individual know that we're sorry for their loss and that if they need anything we are there for them. What happens, however, when we're the grief-stricken person? How do we handle it when we lose something or someone very dear to us? Usually, we want the whole world to come to a dead halt. We want everyone to understand that it's me now and that I'm the one who is hurting.

The Bible tells us to mourn with those who mourn and to rejoice with those who rejoice. Since there is a time to every purpose under the heaven, there are times when we don't feel like laughing; it may be our time to mourn. When we mourn we are expressing sorrow or grief over that which is lost. Most of us have at one time or another experienced the loss of a family member, friend, or acquaintance, and even a favorite pet. It seems as though one day we were talking with them at work or over the phone, laughing at their off-color jokes, enjoying a family picnic or reunion with them, scolding them about bringing over their dirty laundry from the college dorm, enduring their smelly cigars, or complaining because they made the same thing for dinner two days in a row. The next day, they were gone. We'd give anything just to have a few more moments with the loved one. Also, it doesn't matter if the loss is through death, divorce, involuntary separation or departure, or through involuntary separation or departure. The loss still hurts.

No one can tell someone else how to mourn or even how long to mourn. I learned this from Sylvia Petretti who expresses the loss of her son to drugs in her book. *Mark N. Greene, My James Dean*. She was extremely close to her youngest son and his loss would have destroyed her had it not been for the grace of God. Most of us have heard the Bible story of Job, a man who one day had everything: wife, children, wealth, servants, friends, health, and the peace and assurance of God's protection and love. Then one day Job's faith in God was put to the test and he was allowed to lose everything except his life. We speak in admiration about the "patience of Job." However, Job, in his grief, cursed the day he was born. He said he wished he had been as one stillborn. (Job 3:3) Well, most of us experience losses, but not the loss of everything except our lives. Even so, during this time, our very lives seem trivial. At this point in time we feel as though our living has been in vain. We're angry at God; we're angry at the person for leaving us; we're angry at ourselves because we didn't see it coming. We beat ourselves up and repeatedly ask why we didn't prepare for it. We search relentlessly for an answer as to why it happened in the first place.

I can remember experiencing loss so great that I threw the Bible across the room and told God I was no longer going to serve him. If the truth be known, it is during this time that we go through a form of temporary insanity. We are not thinking and acting rationally. Our emotions have taken over and consumed us. It is also the time when we are most vulnerable to illness. Anger will usually die down and give way to depression. This emotion comes when we realize there is nothing we can do to change the situation. Not even our river of tears or our temper tantrums will bring the person or the lost item (tangible or intangible) back to us. Everything starts to seem so unimportant. Sometimes we lose our appetite; other times we eat everything in sight. Temperance has taken a backseat to Excessiveness. We find ourselves at the far end of the spectrum in everything we do. At first, we refrain from visiting certain locations, attending certain events, or engaging in specific types of activities because they remind us of the loved one who is no longer there to enjoy them with us. Then, in an attempt to try and retain some part, however small, of the memory of the loved one, we visit, attend, and engage in those things we were previously so intent on avoiding. This is when well meaning friends and family members tell us that enough is enough. They insist we get on with our lives. In their estimation, we have mourned long enough. After all, it's been "two whole years." We do need our friends and family during this time, but we have to remember that they are not the ones who are experiencing the deep loss that is personal; we are. They, like the friends of Job, think they are doing what is best for us. However, as Job expressed to his friends, "No doubt but ye are the people, and wisdom shall die with you" (Job 12:2).

Nevertheless, we need the people of God. We need the shoulders to cry on, the listening ears, the reassuring words, the heartfelt hugs, and the intercessory prayers. We need to be reminded that "this too shall pass." We need to pray and stay connected to God. He never tires of listening though our friends may grow weary. We need to read his comforting words in the Psalms to remind us that God is our light and our salvation, that he is our shield and buckler, that he is our shepherd who gives us rest, and that we can find safety under his wings and dwell in the place of the Most High, and that we can praise him in good times and in not so good times. We need to rededicate our lives back to God and start reading his word anew and afresh. We need to go back to the cross through the Gospels and the rest of the New Testament to remind us of the one who sacrificed all for us and for our loved one who is no longer there with us, saved and unsaved. If unsaved and still living, we should be driven to our knees on their behalf. If saved and no longer living, remind ourselves that we will see them again if we remain faithful to God. If unsaved and no longer living, we need to remember that the dead do not hear or see or feel. However, we can cherish the memories and the love we had or still have for them.

We need to remember that we, as is the case with all soldiers of war, have been severely wounded, but we will heal. Time has an interesting way of doing just that. When we have healed, we will grow even stronger knowing we have passed one more test of our faith. Before we know it we're, once again, praising God for his goodness and wielding our mighty sword at the enemy and proclaiming with even greater determination, "C'mon Devil, take your best shot!"

Father, I know that not even a sparrow falls to the ground except you notice it. I know that the very hairs on my head are numbered which means you know each and every one. Thank you for a heart to know love and for the time I had with my loved one. Thank you in advance for the healing that, with time, will surely come. I give you praise and glory for all that you are to me. Amen

A Position of Dignity

"The sluggard will not plow by reason of the cold; therefore shall he beg in harvest, and have nothing." Proverbs 20:4

Sometimes I hear people quip, "That guy doesn't know the meaning of work." Perhaps the person in question knows how to define "work"; they just don't care to use it in a sentence, such as, "I work at ...." Of course they're not referring to those, because of the current economic crisis, are unemployed due to loss of a job. They are referring to the "sluggard" who the Bible says needs to be wise and consider the ways of the ant. (Proverbs 6:6) I must say that an ant is by far one of the most interesting insects God created. When I was younger, I used to experiment with them to see what they would do. I would watch them for a while as they scurry in well organized and synchronized fashion. They diligently go about their work with singleness of mind and purpose but in dedication to the group as a whole. I watched as they passed each other, communicating quickly, not missing a beat. They definitely did not believe in idleness, vanity, or office politics. Sadistically, I would wound the legs of one of the workers to see what the insect or the others would do. I was amazed how one of the other workers picked up the wounded worker and proceeded to carry him. What was more amazing is that they recovered from my interference and went back to work.

The same is true when Nehemiah procured permission from the King and dedicated himself to rebuilding the walls of Jerusalem. He planned, organized, gathered materials, and secured diligent workers. Of course, there were antagonists who tried to compromise the work: Sanballot, Tobiah, and Geshem. These are the mockers that try to hinder and stop any work that seems profitable. They even tried to get Nehemiah to come down from the wall, that is, to stop working so hard. However, Nehemiah and his workers turned a deaf ear and kept right on working. We too have our share of Sanballots, Tobiahs, and Geshems. They will tell you not to work so hard. However,

Jesus urged us to work while it is day for the night comes when no man can work, which means we need to redeem the time. (John 9:4) They will tell you they would rather starve than dig ditches or do other menial types of work. Well, rightfully so since the Bible says that a man that does not work should not eat. (2 Thessalonians 3:10) However, if that man has a family and does not take care of them and provide for them, the Bible says that man is worse than an infidel. (1 Timothy 5:8)

It is interesting that people try to use the Genesis account of the Bible to refute the "dignity in all work" maxim (a principle of rule of conduct). They point to the fact that Adam was cursed with having to till the ground by the sweat of his brow to get his food. God said Adam would do this until the day he died. (Genesis 3:17-19) Sounds about right, doesn't it? We work for years and years, then retire, and then really retire: we die. Of course Eve's curse was that she would bear children with much pain in delivering them. (Genesis 3:16) Yes, these were curses due to our original parents' disobedience. However, Jesus delivered us from all curses by his sacrifice. This does not mean, however, we are delivered from having to work. Because of technology, we have managed to save time and minimize the number of hours and the amount of expended energy used to perform our work. However, compared to our Bible patriarchs and matriarchs, we do not live as long, are more tired and unhealthy, and spend a great deal of our conserved time in unprofitable ventures. I've worked ever since I was 9 years old. Of course I had my real summer job when I was a tutor at age 13. However, from age 18 to present I've held way over 40 jobs which include full-time, part-time, temporary, volunteer, and self-employment contracts. My sister has held the one and only job since she was 18 years old. My brother spent a great deal of his life in prison, yet he held several jobs in prison and while out. Of course, in prison he made only a few cents per hour. My mother held several jobs including nurse's aide, welder, and postal worker before she retired. Now, she does volunteer work for her church. My father worked as a cook in the Army, a taxi driver, a truck driver, and operated a driving school before he finally retired. He still works as a volunteer as a computer technician. The common denominator is that we all have worked and continue to work in some form or fashion and there is dignity in all work. We didn't stand near the freeway entrance with a sign with a few misspelled words telling everyone how destitute we are, nor did we look at them sorrowfully to illicit a mixture of guilt and pity that would somehow pry $5, $10, or $20 from their wallets or purses.

There are people who legitimately need temporary help. Jesus said we would always have the poor with us. (Mark 14:7) I should know; I'm one of them. However, the poor can work. They can volunteer in exchange for their meals, clothes, and shelter. This was the original form of exchange before greed set in, capitalism reared its ugly head, big businesses transformed into monster businesses, and the IRS and government became "New World Orderly" big and powerful. So, we all need help temporarily from time to time. When individuals receive temporary help, it's referred to as "welfare." When big businesses receive temporary help, it's referred to as "subsidies." Nevertheless, whatever work we're given to do, whether paid or unpaid, we are to work not as men pleasers, but everything we do, we do it heartily not as unto men, but unto God. (Colossians 3:23)

Lord, I know that it is you who commanded us to work. I know that idle hands are the Devil's workshop. Create in me a diligent and hard-working spirit. Help me to dedicate my time to working for my meals, for my family, for my church, for your service, and not for the Anti-Christ. Amen

---

Weak Ends, Power Begins

"And he said to them, The Sabbath was made for man, and not man for the Sabbath; So that the Son of man is lord even of the Sabbath."
Mark 2:27-28

It's strange that for many years coming up in the church I knew there were things I was told that didn't sit right. Some things didn't quite make sense, but because it was generally accepted, I pushed these gnawing discrepancies aside. It was only until after careful research, seeking God in prayer over what I'd discovered, then more research, and then confirmation in the original language of the Bible, Hebrew and Greek, that I was I finally able to know the truth. The word tells us that one of the jobs of the Holy Spirit is to lead us into all truth. Jesus said that if we ask, seek, and knock, that we would definitely find and receive what we need. This is exactly what the Greeks in Berea did when Paul and Silas preached to them. Paul says these men were nobler than the Hebrews (certain translations call them Jews) in Thessalonica because the Greeks searched the scriptures daily to see if the things they were told were true. Paul says that a number of them had faith. So, do we believe because someone, no matter how well-meaning, told us so, or because we have searched the scriptures for ourselves and know what is true and what is false?

There has been so much controversy over the Sabbath Day. Scholars and laypersons alike have differing views. Some follow it to the letter because it is the law of God. Some find their own interpretation and loopholes. Others disregard it altogether because they believe Jesus treated it with insignificance. One thing I've learned through experience and study with regard to laws is that Supreme Court judges will go back and attempt to determine the founding fathers' intent when the law was enacted. Then they make their ruling based on this determination. We can do the same thing with the 4th Commandment. The Bible, unlike other books, can serve as its own interpreter, since we know that "no prophecy of the scriptures is of any private interpretation" (2 Peter 1:20) and that this prophecy did not come by the will of man, "but holy men of God spake as they were moved by the Holy Ghost" (2 Peter 1:21). So, God does not make mistakes; it is our feeble and finite minds that limit our understanding. We need the help of the "Founding Father" to ensure that we understand the intent of his law. We do not want to be as those who Peter says are unlearned and unstable and "wrest" the scriptures unto our own destruction (2 Peter 3:16).

God intended his law to serve as a schoolmaster to teach us what sin is. Paul says that he would not have understood the true nature of sin except by the law. (Romans 7:7) In Romans 3:23, Paul further explains that we have all sinned and fallen short of the "glory of God." To understand what Paul meant by what was "glorious" we need only read 2 Corinthians 3:7. We understand that the only thing "engraved on stones" was the Law of God, the 10 Commandments. It is the standard, the gauge, to teach us and show us how we measure up to God's righteousness. Jesus said he fulfilled the law; he did not, because he cannot, destroy the law. God's law is like his nature: immutable and unchangeable. In fact, Jesus added emphasis to the commandments that went beyond mere allegiance to the letter of the law. For example, he said that if a man has hatred in his heart for another person, he is guilty of murder in his heart. He said that if a man looks upon a woman to lust after her, not just a mere observance of her beauty, but actual lustful and wanton desire, he has committed adultery with her in his heart. Jesus also emphasized that the Sabbath was made for man, not man for the Sabbath. He kept the Sabbath and he reminded us that it is "lawful to do well on the Sabbath" (Mark 3:4).

So, we know we are commanded to keep the Sabbath and that it is a holy and sacred day. God says six days you work but the seventh day is the Sabbath. One thing to keep in mind is that God is not limited to time and space as we are. However, he accomplished creation in six days, and then he rested on the seventh day from all his work. (Genesis 2:3) God tells us to "remember" the Sabbath day. He commands everyone in your household, including anyone who may be visiting from a foreign country, to observe the Sabbath and to keep it holy. (Exodus 20:8) For God's people, as the Word says, a "day" is from evening (sundown) to morning (sunrise). This means that your Christian friend or relative from Japan, where the time zone is 16 hours ahead of that of the United States, would tell you that his Sabbath day starts while you're still getting your 8 hours of sleep at night. In addition, his Sabbath day ends 8 hours before yours and that he can perform his work. So, which day is the Sabbath?

Most Christians hold Sunday, which is the first day of the week, as the Sabbath. This came about because Jesus rose on the first day of the week which is Sunday and because the Catholic Church and others wanted to distance themselves from anything that was considered Jewish (actually Hebrew). The Hebrews held Saturday as the Sabbath which is the seventh day. Also interesting to note is that there is a "Witches Sabbath" where they worship the Devil. Whatever God establishes, the enemy comes up with counterfeit after counterfeit. Something of extreme importance in understanding God's intent of his law is that he "blessed the Sabbath day and set it apart as holy" (Exodus 20:8-11). God spoke through his prophets who confirmed this. God said "blessed are those who are careful to do this," "blessed are those who honor the Sabbath day by refusing to work," and "blessed are those who keep themselves from doing wrong" (Isaiah 56:2). When God spoke through his prophet Moses, he said that "anyone not honouring it must certainly be put to death" and would be "cut off from his people" (Exodus 31:14).

Death? Cut off? These are harsh words, especially in light of the fact that most of us feel we can choose to honor the Sabbath, not honor it, keep a day other than the day God set apart and made holy, select any day among the seven, or just say, "I keep every day holy" and leave it at that. However, most people who say they keep every day holy are usually not telling the truth; it's impossible to do and God never required it of us.

He just asked us to remember the day he set apart, his special day, to rest from the tedious day to day chores, to receive a blessing from him, and to commune with him. If my mother were to set apart a special day on her calendar to have lunch with me and I showed up the day before, the day after, or just picked any other day of the week to show up, she would not be very happy. Of course I'm sure she would not have me put to death, but we would miss our special time together. We scheduled this time because we are so busy the rest of the week.

Lastly, and more importantly, God spoke through his prophet Ezekiel when he told the people to "keep my Sabbath days holy, for they are sign to remind you that I am the Lord your God" (Ezekiel 20:20). God spoke through his prophet Moses when he said "The people of Israel must keep the Sabbath day forever" because "it is a permanent sign of my covenant with them" (Exodus 31:16). Those of European descent who call themselves Jews are not the true people of Israel. They have lied, robbed, and stolen. There is and never has been a letter "J" in the Hebrew Language. Even the name "Jesus" is actually "Yahoshua." We who are the so-called Negroes are the Black Hebrew Israelites. We are not the Gentiles as our slave masters have taught us. Careful research, prayer, and study of God's word in its original language will reveal such. Also, Paul says that he is not a Hebrew who is one outwardly, but the followers of Christ, though they are Gentiles, have been engrafted in. Whether a Hebrew by birth through generations or by spiritual circumcision of the heart, we are to keep God's Sabbath day forever. It is the permanent sign of God's covenant with us. However, each of us must be persuaded and convicted in our own mind.

The new covenant did not eradicate the first. It merely removed the curse and stain of sin that was upon us. We have our Savior, our Messiah, Jesus (Yahoshua), who is our mediator. Our Savior always did those things that please the Father. Jesus (Yahoshua) rested on the Sabbath day. He rose the next day on

Sunday, ready to "work while it is day." The Law shows us we are guilty. God's grace through faith in Jesus (Yahoshua) paid our fine and we are set free. We are not set free to keep sinning. We are free to repent and turn from our sins to have fellowship once again with God. Because we love our brothers and sisters as ourselves so much that we don't want to lie to them, steal from them, covet what they have, commit adultery with them, kill them without a cause, or dishonor them if they are our parents. Because we love God with all of our heart, mind, soul, and strength, we don't want to have other gods before him, make graven images of other gods and bow down and worship them, take God's name in vain, or forget the Sabbath day to keep it holy. After all, obedience is better than sacrifice (1 Samuel 15:22).

Yahweh, the one and only true God, forgive my limited understanding of your word. Forgive me when I have fallen short of your glory which is your law. I want to worship you in spirit and in truth. I want to keep your Sabbath day holy and I know you made the Sabbath for man and not man for the Sabbath. I am one of your chosen, whether a Black Hebrew Israelite or a born-again Gentile. There is no difference in your sight. We are all saved by your grace. Thank you for the blessing. Thank you for your perpetual sign that you are my God and I am your child forever. Amen

Friend and Foe, Both I Know

"That in blessing I will bless thee, and in multiplying I will multiply thy seed as the stars of the heaven, and as the sand which is upon the sea shore; and thy seed shall possess the gate of his enemies."
Genesis 22:17

I remember when I was a very young I used to always pray that everyone would be happy and have everything they wanted. I understood later that this was impossible; however, my prayer was also selfish. I felt that if everyone was happy they wouldn't treat me so badly. We all have had our share of those who, for whatever reason, have made themselves our enemies. My mother used to tell me that there were four kinds of people in the world: those who like you for the right reasons, those who like you for the wrong reasons, those who dislike you for the wrong reasons, and those who dislike you for the right reasons. She said it was only the last group with which I should concern myself. So, I tried my best not to harm anyone else if I could help it and apologize if I knowingly and unknowingly said or did something to hurt someone physically or emotionally. This worked pretty well; however, it is the third group, those who dislike you for the wrong reasons, who, like the character Glenn Close played in *Fatal Attraction*, "refuse to be ignored" and have tried to make my life a living hell.

Children, teens, and adults who never matured, can be cruel. Because I wore glasses, had a broken front tooth, and was thin as a rail (not considered attractive physical qualities in the poor black community in the late 60's and early 70's), I was teased, ridiculed, and ostracized. Needless to say, I developed an inferiority complex and shied away from joining groups unless they were academic. When added to this scenario the fact that I was a straight-A student and received all kinds of awards (not considered attractive mental qualities in the poor black community in the late 60's and early 70's), I seemed to acquire enemies just by looking at someone too hard. It would be many, many years before I would finally understand that when someone would stare at you and angrily quip, "What are *you* looking at?" it was usually an attempt to intimidate you and to try and cover up his or her own insecurities.

I was never a person given to physical altercations. I was short for my age and more mature than my peers. From age 9 to age 16, I grew up in Compton, California. Gangs never interested me and I couldn't for the life of me understand why kids didn't just discuss their problems rather than assaulting and shooting each other. Two events I remember in particular. One of them was when a neighborhood girl, who I'd played sports with at the park, and a group of other girls, egged us on to fight. It came out of the blue and I didn't learn until later that it was part of her initiation into a gang and to also get me involved. I refused to fight. She pushed me and I yelled at her to leave me alone because I was not going to fight her. She left me alone, the group left, and I assumed she accomplished her goal by challenging someone else who agreed to battle with her because I was sure she was shot and killed many years later. The other event was when I was leaving school after working on the school paper with the Journalism Club. I was feeling good about myself and my accomplishment until three of the girls in the Journalism Club walked behind me and continually pushed me, spouting evil words against me. I stopped dead in my tracks and began to sob vehemently. The only things that were hurt were my feelings. The girls ran away when a teacher came to my rescue. I told her what they had done and they got expelled from school. When I told my mother about it, without missing a beat I lied about how I had responded to the girls. I told my mother I had picked up a stick and hit them to protect myself. My mother was pleased that for once I had stood up for myself. Over the years she repeated my heroism to family and friends. I didn't have the heart to tell her the truth. The worst part was I saw one of the girls again when we moved away from Compton and I graduated to high school. She said hello to me, but I looked at her and did not respond. There was always something deep within me that was ashamed of how childishly I had reacted.

Since that time, I've endured countless displays of rejection, racism, sexism, jealousy, envy, unwarranted revenge, hate words, assault, rape, and other types of trials and persecutions. As a woman of God I know that all who will live Godly in Christ Jesus will suffer persecution (2 Timothy 3:12). Most of the time, this persecution is unwarranted. David, who was appointed as a boy to be successor to King Saul, understood perfectly how you can be hated unjustly even though you fight for the person and try to comfort and please the person. In Psalm 27, David says that when his enemies tried to consume him, they "stumbled and fell" (Verse 2). He says that in time of trouble God hides him "in his tabernacle" and sets him "upon a rock" (Verse 5). He also says that his head is lifted above his enemies so that he can sing praises unto the Lord (Verse 6). Even as king, David had many enemies, outside of his gates and inside his own household. No wonder he sang songs that assured us that: God is our fortress who rescues and saves us from the wicked so that we find shelter in him (Psalm 37:39-40); God will help us do mighty things because he tramples down our foes (Psalm 60:12); and if we love God and hate evil he will rescue us from the power of the wicked (Psalm 97:10).

Protection is not the same as retaliation. We can protect ourselves but vengeance belongs to the Lord. The prophet Isaiah assured us God will leave our enemies confused and ashamed, that anyone who opposes us will be die, that we will look for them and they will be gone, that he is holding us up by his right hand so we have no need to be afraid. (Isaiah 41:11-13) Jeremiah assured us that God himself has spoken and declared that he will rescue us from those we fear and because we trust in God, he will preserve our lives and keep us safe. (Jeremiah 39:17-18) Jesus assured us that God will quickly give justice to his chosen people who plead with him day and night. (Luke 18:7-8) Jesus also assured us that on earth we will have many trials and sorrows but that we should take heart because he has overcome the world. (John 16:33)

In all this, our Lord and Savior tells us not to retaliate when we are persecuted, rather we should pray that God will bless our enemies. He gives us a tall order: to feed our enemies when they are hungry, and to give them water when they are thirsty so they will be ashamed of how they have treated us. (Matthew 5:44) The apostle Paul reiterated this and urged us to bless our enemies and not curse them. (Romans 12:14, 20) Also, we are not to rejoice when our enemies fall into trouble, because God will then be displeased with us and will turn his anger away from our enemies. (Proverbs 24:17-18) Jesus further emphasized doing good to our enemies when he reminded us that God gives sunlight to both the just and the unjust and that he sends rain on the just and the unjust. Jesus says that if we are kind only to our friends how are we different from anyone else. He says even the pagans are kind to their friends. We are a peculiar people. We are the children of God. However, Jesus says that we are to be perfect even as our Father in heaven is perfect. (Matthew 5:45-48)

Father, I am your child, and as such, my ways must be above those who are of this world. Forgive my vengeful thoughts and acts. Help me to see my enemies through your eyes. Help me to pray for them, do well to them when it is my power to do so, tell them about the judgment to come, and when they have repented, tell them about your wonderful plan of salvation. May I always do the things that are pleasing in your sight. Amen

Our Vote of Confidence

"It is better to trust in the Lord than to put confidence in people.
It is better to trust the Lord than to put confidence in princes."
Psalm 118:8-9

Every four years during the second Tuesday in November an event will recur as it has for the last few centuries since America became a nation: the people will go to the polls to vote for their favorite presidential candidate and state senators. Of course this is preceded the year before when we vote for our favorite state and local representatives and certain propositions. However, during the presidential election year most of us can vote for their party candidate between January and June. What this means is that if you're registered as a Democrat, you cannot vote for a candidate who is Republican even though you believe he or she would be best for the job, and vice-versa. People confidently urge you to vote because "it's your civic duty" and "it's your human right." Since America's early beginnings we have been fighting against "taxation without representation." What is amazing is that women and black people had to struggle and fight to gain the same privilege.

There is some good in voting; however we are not to put our trust in it. The operative word in all of politics and government is "control." People want to control the economy, the food source, and every way of life. The masses have become duped into thinking that whoever they put in office, that is, their candidate, will solve the world's problems and make life better for them. No human being is able to do this. The political realm is controlled by Satan and his cohorts. The masses do not put a presidential candidate into office. There is an evil system set up that goes beyond what we could even image. The Bible says there is spiritual wickedness in high places. This is definitely true. In the book of Luke, he describe how the Devil took Jesus to the highest point on earth where he could look down and see all the kingdoms of the world in a moment in time. The Devil told Jesus he would give to him all the glory and authority over these kingdoms, because, the Devil says, they are his to give, if Jesus would just do one thing: bow down and worship the Devil. Of course our Lord and Savior told him, "Get thee behind me Satan; thou shalt worship the Lord thy God and him only shalt thou worship" (Luke 4:8). The Bible says that we are to obey our leaders because God, for whatever reason, allows them to reign. We do well to pray wholeheartedly for them.

We live in this world and we should be concerned about justice and how it is governed. However, we must remember that we are not of this world and that everything here is temporary. We must remember that God, and God alone, governs our lives and his word should govern our actions. It is God who "shatters the plans of the nation and thwarts all their schemes" (Psalm 33:10). Even with the New World Order at our doors, God speaks through his prophet Isaiah in the 40th chapter and tells us that the nations are nothing in comparison to God. He says "they are but a drop in the bucket, dust on the scales and he picks up the islands as though they had no weight at all" (Verse 15) and that the nations are "counted to him less than nothing, and vanity" (Verse 17). The prophet goes on to declare that God will settle international disputes and that all the nations will "beat their swords into plowshares and their spears into pruning hooks" and that "all wars will stop, and military training will come to an end" (Isaiah 2:4). Also, the Bible writers remind us that "all the gods of the nations are idols: but the LORD made the heavens and that honour and majesty are before him: strength and beauty are in his sanctuary" (Psalm 96:5-7).

Jesus reminded us not to seek to be served but to be servants. So, unlike the celebrity status and power we bestow upon government officials. We are not to put our trust in powerful people because there is no help for us there. The Bible says that when their breathing stops, they return to the earth and in a moment their plans come to an end. (Psalm 146:3). However, we are blessed to have the God of Israel as our helper. Our hope should be in God because he is the one who made the heaven and earth, the sea, and everything in them. He is the one who keeps his promises forever. He is the one who gives justice to the oppressed and food to the hungry. He is the one who frees those who are bound, both physically and spiritually. He is the one who opens the eyes of those who are blind. And he is the one who lifts the burdens of those who are bent beneath their heavy loads. Why does he do this? Because he is also the one who loves righteousness. (Psalm 146:3-8).

Finally, when all is said and done, God will judge the system of Antichrist and the Antichrist, along with all those who are partakers of their sins and immorality. America, as a nation, is quickly becoming like the "whore of Babylon" as depicted in the book of Revelations. We have committed adultery with her and our merchants have grown rich as a result. John warns us to "come out from among her" and not to partake of her sins or we will be punished with her. He says God is ready to judge her for her evil deeds and that the sorrows of death and mourning and famine will overtake her in a single day. John says she will be judged by God and she will be utterly consumed by fire. He says the merchants of the world will weep and mourn for her for there is no one left to buy their goods. They will go down in sackcloth and ashes and cry out, "Babylon is fallen – that great city is fallen!" (Revelations 18:1-20). We are God's chosen and we refuse to fall with her.

My Lord, my Alpha and Omega, help me to remember that I merely live in this world which is temporary, but I am not of this world. Forgive me when I put my hope and trust in anything or anyone except for you. Let me cast my vote for truth, justice, and righteousness and let me pray for our leaders that they may be led by nothing or no one else except you. Amen

A Sickness Not Unto Death

"And Jesus went about all the cities and villages, teaching in their synagogues, and preaching the gospel of the kingdom, and healing every sickness and every disease among the people." Matthew 9:35

I remember a comment made by John Amos on the TV show, *Good Times*, as the character, James Evans, whose family was always broke. He said, "Of all things people want to be, being broke is farthest down on the list, just above *sick* and *dead*." It's true that people hate being broke but when they are ill, avoiding death is most on their minds.   Right   now,   I   am praying for my uncle (married to the older of my mother's sisters) who is sick in the hospital but being sent home at his request. I believe he's about 80 years old right now. Over the years he lost his wife to Leukemia and two of his sons to A.I.D.S. One of them lived a homosexual lifestyle before he was saved and the other was an intravenous drug user. His only living son who is also the youngest is married with children and grandchildren. I'm sure he thinks about the possibility that his father may not recover.

When we are ill it is a natural result of a violation of the natural laws that govern our existence. God set everything in order within us and outside of us. Never was a mechanism formed so perfectly and expertly to function and run until it had outlived its purpose. Everything God created he said it was good. We are his crowning glory of creation. We are why the earth, the sea, and all that is them were created. The heavens with its brightly lit stars and moon to give us light in the night season, and the brightness of the sun to give us light and warmth during the day, were created just for us. The herbs, fruits, and vegetation on the earth were created to nourish us. The natural spring water created to replenish the 75% of which our bodies are made. Even the very air we breathe comes from the vegetation created for us. God made sure that an even exchange would take place to sustain our existence. We breathe in oxygen (O_2) from the atmosphere and give off carbon dioxide (CO_2) expelled from our lungs. The carbon dioxide is taken in by the vegetation that gives off oxygen (O2). We consume fruits and vegetation and water complete with the necessary elements and compounds that we need to sustain our existence. In return, we expel the items that we consider as "wastes" back into the earth and atmosphere. These wastes are utilized and converted as nutrients for the vegetation and atmosphere. Animals were created so Adam could practice his dominion and to keep him company. God had high hopes for mankind because, unlike the animals, God put within us the ability to think and reason. However, due to sin, we have learned to think and reason ourselves out of existence.

God gave Moses specific and detailed instructions to the people to govern every aspect of their lives. Even the minutest attention was given to laws concerning diet, cleansing, and waste elimination. All of God's instructions were to keep man healthy, vital, and free from sickness and disease. Of course, as time went on, people began to violate and disregard these laws. Man's years grew shorter and shorter, especially after the flood when they began to consume animals. You are what you eat. If you want to live you eat live vegetation. It was never intended for us to consume flesh but God allowed it. As Paul says, "All things are lawful unto me, but all things are not expedient" (1 Corinthians 6:12; 10:23). Drinking coffee and sodas, smoking cigarettes and cigars, and eating sugar and other foods containing man-made chemicals, will not send you to hell, but they can seriously impair your God-given immune system. God is intelligent in his design of our bodies, so much so, that our bodies have the ability to heal themselves. When one cell dies, another has already begun to replace it. Every seven years all of the cells renew themselves. In fact, there is absolutely no logical reason, at least from our finite mental understanding, why the human body begins to age, eventually lose its immune system altogether, and eventually dies. The only God-given explanation is that God set it in motion to be so. Because of man's original sin, God honored his word when he told Adam and Eve that the day they partake of the tree of good and evil they would die. (Genesis 2:16-17)

Of course, God's plan of salvation through Jesus was already set in motion before he spoke those words. He knows everything from beginning to end. We may ask why this and why that. We can do this to our own end and complete insanity. Man only uses a small percentage of his intellectual capacity, which means God has given us what we need to understand within these physical houses. He will give us spiritual bodies if we endure to the end. These bodies will never get ill and, therefore, will never die. The new heaven and new earth will be created expertly and perfectly to sustain our existence. Our temporal existence here on earth is but for a moment. Our lives wither away like the green grass. (Psalm 37:2) Even a thousand years is but a drop in the bucket compared to eternity. We try to obey God's written, physical, and spiritual laws as best we can. However, as sin-sick souls who are saved by grace, we are terminally ill. Yet, thanks to our Lord and Savior and his death on the cross, this sickness is not unto death.

Powerful Creator, thank you for my very life and everything you have created to sustain my life. Help me to understand, accept, and obey the laws you have established. I know they were given out of your love for me. When I become ill, give me the knowledge to use what you have created for my healing and give me the serenity to wait patiently on you. Amen

To Know Even As I Am Known

And thou, Solomon my son, know thou the God of thy father, and serve him with a perfect heart and with a willing mind: for the LORD searcheth all hearts, and understandeth all the imaginations of the thoughts: if thou seek him, he will be found of thee; but if thou forsake him, he will cast thee off forever." I Chronicles 28:9

Ever since my children were born I tried to attend to their every need. When they were babies they could not talk, so I learned to listen to and distinguish from their different cries. I learned to read their body language and interpret their smiles, and more importantly, I could read their eyes which are the windows to the soul. I fed them, bathed them, played games with them, taught them, read bedtime stories to them, spoiled them, and pampered them. When I was not at work, I spent quality time with them and combed and brushed their hair at night until they went to sleep sucking on a bottle of milk. As my children grew they learned to talk and began to communicate verbally. They had listened and learned from their father and me and from the environment around them. They started utilizing all of the nurturing they had received. Since I divorced when they were young, they spent the majority of their years and time with me. People knew they were mine not just because they looked like their father and me, but also because they sounded like me, their mannerisms were like mine, the inflections in their voices were like mine, their laugh was like mine, and even their way of viewing life was like mine.

My children got to know me. They knew they could come to me when they were hurting or in trouble. They knew they could talk to me about anything and I would listen, even when they did something wrong. Of course, my son would lie and my daughter would cover up things. I would always find out and I would discipline them. They would look at me with their sorrowful brown eyes and I would forgive them. However, they knew they would have to face the consequences of their actions, and there was never any doubt in their minds that I loved them and cared about them. They went through their periods of rebellion but when they grew into adulthood they saw themselves and their lives through my eyes. They began to appreciate the time we spent, the learning, the discipline, the games, and the communication we had and continue to have, especially when my son married and had his own children. In other words, because of the time we spent, we all grew to know and understand each other.

We are God's children whom he cares for, nurtures, and loves. We were born again into his family. As spiritual converts, we are forever allowing him to teach us. We commune and communicate with him through prayer. Our prayers can be audible or inaudible. They can be spoken or unspoken. They can be short or long. They can even be unintelligible groaning in our spirit. They can come through tears or through laughter. Our prayers can be petitions or requests. They can be prayers for guidance and direction. They can be prayers of thanksgiving and praise. They can be prayers of worship and adoration to God for who he is. The psalmists tell us that: "The LORD is nigh unto all them that call upon him, to all that call upon him in truth. He will fulfill the desire of them that fear him: he also will hear their cry, and will save them." (Psalm 145:18-19) God declared through his prophet Isaiah: "And it shall come to pass, that before they call, I will answer; and while they are yet speaking, I will hear." (Isaiah 65:24) God spoke through his prophet Jeremiah and assured the people: "For I know the thoughts that I think toward you, saith the LORD, thoughts of peace, and not of evil, to give you an expected end. Then shall ye call upon me, and ye shall go and pray unto me, and I will hearken unto you. And ye shall seek me, and find me, when ye shall search for me with all your heart." (Jeremiah 29:11-13)

Jesus taught us how to pray (Luke 11:1). He taught us where to pray (Matthew 6:6). He taught us with what motives to pray (Matthew 6:7). He taught us to continually ask, seek, and knock in faith and that our prayers would be answered (Matthew 7:7-8). He urged us to stay connected to him, the vine, and for his words to abide in him, for if we do this and ask anything according to God's will, we will have whatever we ask (John 15:4). In other words, we can come boldly to the throne of grace and ask our loving parent for anything at anytime and we will find the help and answers we need (Hebrews 4:16). However, God is holy. He will not hear the prayers of those who sin without repentance, but we know that the prayers of a righteous man, he who has right standing with God, avails much (James 5:16). Therefore, Jesus tells us that if we have unforgivingness in our hearts for others or if we know that someone has "ought" against us, we must first go and be reconciled to them and then return to the altar to offer our prayers (Mark 11:24-25; Matthew 5:23).

We don't have to worry about anything. We can have peace once we have put everything at the Lord's feet. God hears every prayer and he answers every prayer. Sometimes the answer is "yes," sometimes the answer is no, and sometimes the answer is simply "to wait." One thing to remember is that God will not go contrary to his word. This is the solidifying part of communication with God. When we pray, we're talking with him; when we read his word, he's talking with us. Communication is a two-way process. As a loving parent, God knows us through and through. We must spend time in his word and get to know him. We need to allow him to feed us, teach us, instruct us, discipline us, and help us to grow into spiritual maturity. No matter what spiritual age we reach, we can remain confident and assured that those loving arms are there to welcome us and those grace-filled hands are there with good things to help us prosper and to pick us up when we fall. Our constant communion and communication with our loving Father through prayer and his word will always guide us back home.

> *Abba Father, thank you for the gift of prayer. Thank you that I can lay all things at your feet. Thank you that I can ask what I need with confidence that you will provide it. Thank you for being my protector, my provider, and my constant companion. May I pray without ceasing and may your word change me into your image from glory to glory. Amen*

True Fellowship

"And let us consider one another to provoke unto love and to good works: Not forsaking the assembling of ourselves together, as the manner of some is; but exhorting one another: and so much the more, as ye see the day approaching." Hebrews 10:24-25

There was a time, in my ignorance, when I went to church just to listen to the choir sing. One of the men told me that if he ever got to that point, he would just stop going at all. He said church was more than that. I had experienced so much heartache with other people who were not saved; however, I was devastated to experience even worse among those who called themselves saved. It was enough to make a person head for the hills at the very mention of church. After studying the word and deciding not to "throw the baby out with the bathwater," I discovered that there are some wolves in sheep clothing in the church. In other words, they are in the church but the church is not in them. However, I discovered that there are also good, praying, and loving truly saved people in the church. Sometimes they took my children and I out to eat, sometimes they invited us to their homes to eat and fellowship, they donated used clothing, helped fix my car when it went out, gave me rides to church or to the grocery store when needed, gave me what few dollars they could spare, and were always there with a kind word or prayer. It is through them that I witnessed the love of Christ in action.

It is true that there are no solitary Christians. We are all a part of one body. The apostle Paul likens the church to the human body with its many parts. Just as the human body has parts with different functions, so too does the body of Christ, the church. However, we all have one purpose and are governed by the same Holy Spirit. (1 Corinthians 10:16-17) Each part is to care for the others, protect the others, and be alert when one part is in distress, just as pain is the distress signal to alert the brain and the rest of the parts of the body that something is wrong. In addition, no one part is greater or more important than another. When one part suffers, all of us suffer; when one part is exalted, all of us are exalted. (1 Corinthians 12:13-20) When one of us is caught in some sin, we are not to condemn the person, but gently and humbly help the person back onto the right path, considering ourselves lest we fall into the same kind of temptation. (Galatians 6:1-3)

Most of the time, the body functions well. We see congregations today, as in the early church, with those who don't just talk the talk, but they also walk the walk. They know that fellowship with other believers is not just having that comforting feeling of companionship and closeness during services, but it also means rolling up their sleeves and putting their faith into action. The Bible says that the people met together constantly and shared everything they had. They even sold their possessions and shared with those who had need. There was no poverty, no DES office, no social welfare, no AFDC, no TANF, no food stamps, no food cards, and no one standing on the freeway with "Will Work for Food" signs. God honored their efforts because they did this without complaining and murmuring. Instead, they praised God. (Acts 2:44-47; 4:32-35). The people genuinely loved each other and honored each other. In fact, they invited guests home and gave them lodging if they needed it.

When God gives us a word, it convicts us first. I am reminded of a few years ago when family members were coming to town for my uncle's funeral. He was married to my mother's younger sister. He never survived the cancer treatments. My mother, without asking me, had already arranged for the children and grandchildren of the family members to stay at my house while the family members who were my age would stay at her home. I resented this because I kept thinking I would end up babysitting and felt I didn't have enough supplies for them, nor did I believe my accommodations were as nice as my mother's. The visiting family never talked with me and never got to hear my reservations. I guess it didn't matter. They ended up getting a hotel room for $50 for the night. I was pricked in my spirit and remorseful. Regardless of the situation, I had room to accommodate them, and I asked God for forgiveness. Unfortunately, as such is the case, I never asked for theirs. I never truly communicated with them. My communication with God means nothing without communication with other believers.

So, there are times, as in my case noted above, when the body dysfunctions due to faulty parts. I think the apostle James said it best, "If a brother or sister be naked, and destitute of daily food, And one of you say unto them, Depart in peace, be ye warmed and filled; notwithstanding ye give them not those things which are needful to the body; what doth it profit?" (James 2:15-16) The apostle goes on to say that we are believers, it's true, but the Devil is also a believer; he knows that there is one God just as we do. However, as James explains that one person can say he has faith and another says he has works. One may be able to show the other his faith without works, but the other can show him his faith by his works. In other words, "faith without works is dead." (James 2:18-20) Faith by works is true fellowship.

> *My Lord and Savior, the author and finisher of my faith, and the first fruits of the brethren — forgive my times of ignorance and times when I have failed to meet the needs of my brothers and sisters in Christ. I know that I will give an account for this. I pray for a renewed obedient and generous spirit that is led by your word and your all-knowing Holy Spirit. Amen*

The Greatest of Gifts

"Even so ye, forasmuch as ye are zealous of spiritual gifts, seek that ye may excel to the edifying of the church." I Corinthians 14:12

A gift is something you did not earn or merit. Usually, it is appreciated more if it is something you did not buy for yourself. With baited breath and heartfelt expectation, I watch each time my parents, my siblings, my spouse, my children, or my friends open up a special gift that I had given them. Oh, the joy that elates my heart when I see their eyes light up in surprise and the grateful smiles and hugs that assure me that I made the right choices. Sometimes the gifts are not always the right ones: they are the wrong color, the wrong size, or one that totally missed the mark and I find out later has been donated to Goodwill. However, unlike the gifts we give, God never makes mistakes.

God is big on giving. He gave the world his only son so we can have eternal life, not because we were good people, but because we weren't. This gift is called grace and cannot be earned nor can it be bought. God always has a purpose in the gifts he gives. When Jesus had served his earthy purpose, God took the gift away and replaced him with another gift. He gave us the gift of the Holy Spirit. It is not something we can earn, buy, or bargain for. It is not something for which we need to tarry. Jesus told his disciples to tarry, that is to wait, in the city of Jerusalem until they were imbued with power from on high. (Luke 24:49) The disciples did as Jesus had instructed them to do. On that great day of Pentecost when all the believers were on one accord and in agreement, God fulfilled his promise spoken by Jesus. He sent another comforter that today imbues each repentant and born-again believer with power from on high and leads us into all truth. With the "sound from heaven as of a mighty rushing wind," he sent the Holy Ghost, that baptism of fire, which manifested itself that day as "cloven tongues like as of fire" that sat upon each and every believer in "the upper room" (Acts 2:1-3). There were devout people from every nation that day; they spoke in other tongues as the Spirit gave them utterance, each heard in his or her own language, and they witnessed and testified to the glory of God (Acts 2:4).

People marveled then as they do today when they witness the goodness of God whose gifts are without repentance, and whose goodness leads us to repentance. (Romans 2:4) The unsaved could not help asking what they must do to be saved, and Peter, who at one time denied his Lord and Savior three times as predicted, was the first to speak up: "Repent, and be baptized every one of you in the name of Jesus Christ for the remission of sins, and ye shall receive the gift of the Holy Ghost." (Acts 2:38) The Holy Ghost is our down payment from heaven. We know that we belong to him and have the right to our inheritance. The deal has been sealed and God will deliver as promised. Even though we do not yet have the physical manifestation, God has given the Holy Ghost as the divine key that opens up other gifts to use while we wait and to prepare ourselves and others for that great moving day. He gave us Spiritual Gifts.

A Spiritual Gift is a special divine empowerment given to every believer by the Holy Ghost to accomplish a given ministry God's way according to his grace and discernment to be used within the context of the Body of Christ. However, a Spiritual Gift is not the same as a natural talent or ability. It goes beyond these abilities and can be recognized in three ways: 1) the gifted person will be more effective in it; 2) the gifted person will tend to devote more time and energy to it than a person who is not gifted in this manner; and 3) the gifted person will see greater results more consistently while engaging in that activity than those without the Spiritual Gift. Also, unlike a natural talent or ability, a Spiritual Gift has the Holy Spirit as its source.

Every believer has at least one Spiritual Gift, but some have many. God distributes severally as he wills. It is not the number of gifts you receive or even which gifts you receive that matters most to God. However, he does care that you do use your gift and how you use your gift. This is illustrated in one of the parables Jesus told his disciples regarding to what the kingdom of heaven could be likened. He told the story about a man who traveled away from home and gave talents (goods or gifts) to his servants. To one he gave five, to another two, and to another he gave only one. Jesus said that the ones to whom he gave five and two talents utilized them and increased them, that is, they became fruitful. However, the one who received only one talent hid it and left it idle so that no one prospered by it. Jesus said that the servant with only one unused talent will be taken away from him who Jesus called "slothful" and given to those who had increased their talents. Jesus also warned us that "unprofitable servants" will be cast "into other darkness" and that there would be "weeping and gnashing of teeth." (Matthew 25:14-30) In other words, we will be held highly accountable.

The Bible says that the spiritual gifts come in different forms, manifestations, and administrations. Some have the gift of teaching, some preaching, some prophecy, some healing, some hospitality, and of course there are a multitude of others. The spiritual gifts were given for the building up and edifying of the body of Christ, for the work of the ministry, and the perfecting (spiritual cosmetology) of believers. (Ephesians 4:12) How long are we to keep our gifts? Remember, God never takes something away we need unless he replaces it with something else. The Bible tells us that we are to keep the Spiritual Gifts and use them "until we all reach unity in the faith and in the knowledge of the Son of God and become mature, attaining to the whole measure of the fullness of Christ." (Ephesians 4:13) Anyone who is in tuned with the body of Christ knows that we have not reached this point. There is a time when God will remove his Spirit, but when he does, he will send Jesus back to receive us, that is, the bridegroom will return for his bride, the church. The Bible says, "the Lord himself shall descend from heaven with a shout, with the voice of the archangel, and with the trump of God: and the dead in Christ shall rise first: Then we which are alive and remain shall be caught up together with them in the clouds, to meet the Lord in the air: and so shall we ever be with the Lord." (1 Thessalonians 4:16-17) A new heaven and earth will God create; we will live on earth with Christ who will reign on his throne. This is the only time when the Spiritual Gifts will no longer be needed, for the Best Gift of All will be returned to us and for us.

> *Father in Heaven, the great giver of gifts — I thank you for the gift of life and the resources you bestow. I thank you for your spiritual gifts. Please make my gifts known to me and teach me how to use them for your glory. Forgive me when I hide my light under a bushel. Help me to appreciate the gifts of others and to work in harmony with them to build up and edify the body of Christ. Amen*

Chasing the Wind

"I returned, and saw under the sun, that the race is not to the swift, nor the battle to the strong, neither yet bread to the wise, nor yet riches to men of understanding, nor yet favour to men of skill; but time and chance happeneth to them all." Ecclesiastes 9:11

Ever watch a dog chasing his tail? I marvel as the dog goes round and round. We laugh because he looks silly. We know that it's a meaningless pursuit. However, what about when we chase the wind? This pursuit is void of purpose. We cannot catch the wind because it is forever intangible. We see its short-lived effects and then it moves on. We do not see from where it comes and we do not know to where it goes. When I was younger I had an inferiority complex. I didn't look, think, and act like TV and movies said I'm supposed to. Of course, this was further iterated by family and friends who were also products of the idiot box, the tube that creates couch potatoes and brain-washed clones, and Hollywood, the place that "creates magic" and illusions of real life. Of course there are times when these mediums can and do teach us important truths. However, during any one TV program, every 10-15 minutes a commercial reminds us that we won't get a date with dandruff, dull teeth, sweaty armpits, and bad breath. In fact, to be accepted, we absolutely must wear certain clothes, shoes, and accessories. Also, anybody who's anybody must drive certain cars, dwell in specific homes, live within certain communities, network within certain circles of influence, vacation at specific resorts and countries, and earn a certain amount of money. So, we spend our time in pursuit of these things or worrying about how to obtain them.

None of the pursuits mentioned above can satisfy. Not only are they temporal, but the so-called standards keep changing and people are left chasing their tails. The best example would be the character, Tony Montana, played by Al Pacino in the 1983 movie *Scarface*. He and his friends immigrated to the States in search of the American Dream. Most kids seem to remember him holding his machine gun and uttering, "Say hello to my little friend," and shooting up as many of the "bad guys" as possible. However, I'll never forget his words to his friend and his wife, after he'd engaged in drugs, theft, murder, and other unlawful acts trying to obtain wealth and all the great things it could buy: he said, "This is it? This is what it's all about?" The wife he'd killed and stolen for could not even bare him children. The image at the end of the movie shows him lying dead in the huge swimming pool of his mansion below the high-rise marquee of glittering words, "I'm on top of the world." Tony Montana had been fiercely and futility chasing the wind.

A much wiser, wealthier, and world-renown God-fearing man, named Solomon, did not pillage and murder; however, he too chased the wind. Solomon engaged in every kind of activity, delicacy, and endeavor there was on the face of the earth during his time. He found that everything he worked so hard to accomplish was meaningless. He found that people were motivated to succeed by their envy of their peers and neighbors. He said it was like chasing the wind. (Ecclesiastes 2:11; 4:4) Solomon discovered that there were some serious problems. He said people hoard up riches to the harm of those who do so, people make risky investments that are sometimes lost with nothing to pass on to their children, and people who live for wealth come to the end of their lives as naked and empty-handed as the day they were born. He says that all their hard work is for nothing because it is temporal and will eventually be swept away. He says that because of this, people live their lives under a cloud where they are frustrated, discouraged, and angry. (Ecclesiastes 5:13-17) Solomon concluded that apart from God, "all is vanity." (Ecclesiastes 1:14) In other words, without God, life is meaningless. Finally, Solomon declared, "Let us hear the conclusion of the whole matter: Fear God, and keep his commandments: for this is the whole duty of man." (Ecclesiastes 12:13

Our self-esteem should not come from how we look, how much money we make, what kind of cars we drive, how many degrees we hold, what great feats we accomplish, or even what other people think of us. Our self-esteem only depends on how God sees us. (1 Corinthians 4:3-4) Jesus reminded us that a sparrow has much less worth than a man, yet not one of them falls to the ground without God's notice, and we are more valuable to God than they are. (Matthew 10:29-31) He said that because we are God's people, we are "the salt of the earth" (Matthew 5:1). He meant we are like salt which the body requires to removes toxins and increases the memory and functioning of the brain. Jesus said we are "the light of the world" and should never hide this light but allow our good works to shine so that God will be glorified (Matthew 5:14-16). The apostle Peter reminds us that we are a chosen people, a kingdom of priests, God's holy nation, and God's very own possession. He reminds us that this is so that we can bear witness to the goodness of God and show how he called us "out of darkness into his marvelous light." (1 Peter 2:9) So when we boast, as the apostle Paul says, we should boast only of what God has done. (2 Corinthians 10:17) Paul of all people understood that in our weakness we are made strong. (2 Corinthians 12:7-10) Therefore, we have no need to compare ourselves with others.

Like the psalmist in Psalm 139, we can praise God because he loved us and cared for us even before we were born, he took great care in knitting our bodies together perfectly, he places his hands of blessing upon our heads, and no matter where we go, his hand guides us and supports us with his strength. We too can declare, "How precious also are thy thoughts unto me, O God! How great is the sum of them!" (Psalm 139:17). Then, finally, we can stop chasing the wind and agree with the apostle Paul who, though in chains, a prisoner locked up and persecuted for his faith, declared with all his might, "But what things were gain to me, those I counted loss for Christ. Yea doubtless, and I count all things but loss for the excellency of the knowledge of Christ Jesus my Lord: for whom I have suffered the loss of all things, and do count them but dung, that I may win Christ, and be found in him, not having mine own righteousness, which is of the law, but that which is through the faith of Christ, the righteousness which is of God by faith." (Philippians 3:8-9)

> *My God, I know that there is nothing in this world for which I strive that will satisfy my need. I know that my worth does not depend on anything except what you think of me. Help me to let go of feelings of worthlessness and to see myself through your eyes. Thank you for your love, care, and strength. Amen*

Finishing the Race

"But he that shall endure unto the end, the same shall be saved."
Matthew 24:13

Everyone of us at one time of another has started off gung-ho about a project where we are ready to tackle the world, and because of obstacles or barriers that rear their ugly heads, we find ourselves hindered and sometimes, stopping the project altogether. Sometimes I think about the plight of those of African descent and everything Black people have had to overcome from slavery to civil rights to affirmative action to now when it is almost the year 2011 and so many of those struggles and accomplishments are being reversed. In spite of it all, I cannot help but marvel at the tenacity and perseverance of a people, who by all intents and purposes, should have succumbed a long time ago to the blatant attempts of genocide and total annihilation. A great number of Jews persevered and survived despite Hitler's desire to see them extinguished from the face of the earth. Of course other races have had their share of struggles and countless war stories. One thing that is central to all is the desire to persevere come what may.

People who intentionally commit suicide are cowards. Not only is it a sin in God's eyes to take a life, even our own, because it does not belong to us, but it takes courage to stand in the midst of the storms of our lives. When everything is going fine and there are no problems, it's easy to travel along happily in our new Victory Van, complete with its new glory paint, its engine gassed up with zeal and filled to the brim with oil of gladness, its automatic transmission operating on grace and mercy, its gospel horn to let everybody know when we're in town, its handles from heaven of doors that no man can open or shut without God's approval, its windshield of faith to protect against the elements, and its wheels of worship to keep us rolling along and praising God. We feel spiritually motivated to travel miles and miles on the road of salvation. However, sooner or later, in fact more sooner than later, we hit several bumps in the road, run out of gas, have a flat tire, our horn stops working, our engine stalls, our transmission has not been tuned up for a while, and someone has crashed into us, causing our glory paint to peel. Yet, we still have miles and miles to go. This is where the rubber meets the road, so to speak. The thrill is gone and a great number of us fail to complete our destination.

It is during these times that our faith is put to the test and we learn what we're made of. The apostle James encourages us to count it all joy when we enter these types of trials and struggles because the trying of our faith works patience, and once patience has completed its work we will be complete and lack nothing. (James 1:2-4) He further states that we are truly blessed if we endure testing with patience because in so doing, we will receive the crown of life that God has promised to those who love him. (James 1:12) It is a truth that all who will live godly in Christ Jesus will suffer persecution, but if we endure our hardships we will reign with God. (2 Timothy 3:12; 2:12) Sometimes these trials and hardships can tend to discourage us, but God assured us through the apostle Paul that though we are "slaughtered like sheep all the day long," victory in Christ Jesus is ours. Paul says he is convinced, as we should be, that "nothing can separate us from the love of God." Not even life or death, angels or demons, our fears of today or worries of tomorrow, principalities or powers, highest places or lowest places, or anything in creation can separate us from the love of God that is revealed in Christ Jesus. (Romans 8:35-38) Jesus promised us that no one would be able to snatch us away from him because he gives us eternal life which means we will not perish. (John 10:28-29)

Therefore, we should never get tired of well doing, nor should we get discouraged and give up. God promises blessings for those who endure. (Galatians 6:9) We need only keep our focus on the end goal and what we are trying to achieve. Our goal is to pass the tests here on earth. God wants to see if we can be trusted with eternity. Paul reminds us that there is going to be a day of judgment when God will judge everyone according to what they have done. God will give eternal life to those who persist in doing good, and who seek after glory and honor and immortality. (Romans 2:5-7) We can rest assured that God will deliver us from every evil attack and will bring us safely to his heavenly kingdom. (2 Timothy 4:18) We need only be faithful unto the end and trust God when we hit the bumps on the road just as firmly and strongly as we did when we first believed. If we do, we will share in all that belongs to Christ. (Hebrews 3:14). We will eat from the tree of life in the paradise of God. (Revelation 2:7) There is a song that says, *"Take me back. Take me back, Dear Lord, to the place where I first received you. Take me back. Take me back, Dear Lord, where I first believed."* With these words in mind, we can always focus on our end goal by remembering why we are traveling on this journey in the first place.

Dear Lord, though at times I grow weary and may feel discouraged, continue to shine your light on the path of my journey. I know you have no pleasure in those who turn back in disbelief. Help me to persevere and to press forward. Thank you for the knowledge and confidence that not only are you with me but that nothing will separate me from you. I vow to keep moving ahead toward victory. Amen

Unwelcomed Guests

"And they were all amazed, and spake among themselves, saying, What a word is this! for with authority and power he commandeth the unclean spirits, and they come out." Luke 4:36

When we speak of being possessed by demons, the first image that comes to most people's minds is Linda Blair in the *Exorcist*. We picture a creature with distorted features levitating, puking up green liquid, cursing, speaking in Latin or backwards in English, and their heads turning all of the way around. Demonic spirits are real but we must remember that Satan can appear as an angel of light. (2 Corinthians 11:14) The Devil has learned the art of deception so well that if were possible he would fool the very elect. This is how serial rapists and murderers have been able to claim victim after victim. They look like "the boy next door." They are polite and have unassuming dispositions; we think to ourselves, "He (or she) wouldn't hurt a fly." However, these people have become possessed of the Devil. They have allowed him to take up residence within them and use them for the Devil's own diabolical ends. We know Satan is a liar and the father of lies, there is no truth in him, and he seeks to steal, kill, and destroy.

I've had several knowing encounters with demonic forces, with people who were inhabited by demonic spirits, and with those who were outright witches. The first time was when I was a child. I woke up in the middle of the night to find one of the little imps hovering over me about to touch me. I sat up and gasped, and it scampered away and disappeared from my sight. I never told my parents because they would have said I was just dreaming. I know that over the years my guardian angel has been protecting me from events and situations of which I have been totally unaware. For that I am truly thankful. However, there have been people filled with demonic spirits who have tried and did hinder my spiritual walk and shake my confidence. I remember a woman and daughter from whom my children and I rented a small room. There was no door to the room and we were always visited at night by a deranged cat. I had to put furniture in the door to prevent the cat from entering and frightening my children. The woman's boyfriend and she used to put ice cubes in the form of phallic symbols to see how I would react. I ignored their childish behavior.

I remember another time when a sister in Christ and I were visiting one of the single church members to pray for her and her children. While we were praying, one of the visiting neighborhood kids opened her eyes and looked up at me and I recognized the devilish smile. She said, "Are you Jesus' wife?" Then she began to giggle. There was another young boy who was the son of a woman with whom I accompanied to a special gospel play at a church in northeast Phoenix. The child was unruly, cursed his mother, and said that he "hated God." It seems not many parents want to believe their child needs to be healed of demonic spirits. Instead, they want to believe that he or she is ADHD and just needs more drugs.

At one time I was ensnared into a sexual relationship with a man who I thought to be a man of God but who was, in reality, possessed with a legion of devils. He confessed that he'd committed murder but gave me no details. Years before that, I had a sexual relationship with a man who confided in me that he was a "white witch." Apparently, this meant he was a "good witch," however, I knew that he'd committed murder but I had no proof. It is important to note that these demons keep tabs on the people of God. They try their best to catch you at your lowest point. They know just what temptations will most likely ensnare you. Without the armor of God, you are spiritual prey.

The most amazing encounter that I remember is when a handful of us were praying for a woman who was possessed of many demonic spirits. The demons identified themselves and spoke. They said they were going to kill her husband and then kill her. The woman was delivered and healed and became a mighty woman of God. Since that time, I've been able to "see" the demonic spirits in the eyes and on the countenances of people. One of my Spiritual Gifts is discerning of spirits. I can usually tell if someone or something is of God or of the Devil. The problem ensues when that individual deceives the people around them, including members of the church. It takes prayer and fasting to be directed of God in how to act. Jesus said there are many wolves in sheep clothing, but we have to allow the "tares" and the "wheat" to grow together. He said he would separate them at harvest time. We can, however, allow the Word of God to convict their consciences. We can rebuke their overt and covert actions and words that are contrary to God's law and his word.

Other than demons speaking to us outright, we can detect when someone needs to be delivered. The Devil uses sex because this drive is so powerful that it creates life. Any person involved in any unnatural or deviant sexual behavior such as adultery, fornication, homosexuality, sadism, pedophilia, or sodomy, is, for all intents and purposes, practicing the spirit of witchcraft. These perverted sexual acts are flags that the individual is living in deception. Next, if any person espouses beliefs that are contrary to the expressed written word of God, understood in its cultural and historical context, and teaches that the Bible and God's Law is not the standard to which we should measure ourselves, is a liar and the truth is not in him or her. We need to, however, study to show ourselves approved so that we can rightly divide the word of truth. (2 Timothy 2:15) Lastly, another key sign of demonic possession is a person who constantly stirs up disharmony and confusion. This person will constantly cause brethren to be at odds due to mischief he has sown and sits back and laughs at them.

The Bible warns us to "lay hands suddenly on no man." (1 Timothy 5:22) We should always give people time to prove themselves. We judge too quickly by looks and smooth words. However, the Bible says that "a naughty person, a wicked man, walks with a forward mouth," and he "winks with his eyes, speaks with his feet, and teaches with his fingers" (Proverbs 6:12-13). In addition, he continually "devises mischief" and "sows discord" (Proverbs 6:14). God says that, in addition to these things, God hates "a proud look, a lying tongue, and hands that shed innocent blood." (Proverbs 6:17) These actions are also flags that tells when a person is possessed of spirits and needs deliverance, for the Bible says that we will "know them by their fruits," that is, by their actions. (Matthew 7:16)

Although the Devil and his angels (demons) are powerful, they are no match for the people of God. Jesus recognized demons, silenced them, and then cast them out with his authoritative words. The demons know who we are and they tremble. Jesus told his disciples that he "saw Satan falling from heaven as a flash of lightning," and Jesus gave them "authority over all the power of the enemy," so much so that they could "walk among snakes and scorpions and crush them," and that "nothing will injure" them. (Luke 10:18-19) However, Jesus told them not to rejoice that the spirits were subject them, but that they should rejoice because their "names are written in heaven." (Luke 10:20). Therefore, we need to be discerning, but need not fear. We need only submit ourselves unto God, resist the Devil and the Devil will flee." (James 4:7) We can surely do this because "God hath not given us the spirit of fear; but of power, and of love, and of a sound mind." (James 4:1)

> Wise and Holy Father, thank you for your Holy Spirit and for your power from on high. Thank you that demons are subject unto you and your kingdom. Help me to recognize the enemy and his forces. Help me to break down his strongholds and speak words of deliverance. Thank you Lord, most of all, for eternal life. Amen

A Backsliding Atheist

"The fool hath said in his heart, There is no God. They are corrupt,
they have done abominable works, there is none that doeth good."
Psalm 14:1

There is a saying that, "There are no atheists in foxholes." However, I know there are no true atheists – period. Ray Comfort, a writer and evangelist, shows how easy it is to make an atheist backslide. When confronted with real truths and logic, the professing atheist discovers that their beliefs are based on shaky and unproven assumptions. They are left mumbling words and phrases to themselves such as "maybe," "probably," and "I really don't know." They discover that they are not truly atheists; they are actually agnostics. To prove that God exists, one need only examine a painting. The fact that the painting exists proves that there must have been a painter. If we look at a building, we know the fact that the building exists proves that there must have been a builder. In the same way, when we look at creation, we know the fact that creation exists proves there must have been a creator. This is pure and simple logic.

Some people, on the other hand, believe in the Big Bang Theory. This theory is based on the belief that some unknown cosmic explosion took place for some unknown reason and a highly organized and perfectly designed galaxy, complete with highly ordered interdependent planetary systems, just appeared one day. However, usually the "bangers" also believe in the Theory of Evolution and that man evolved from amphibians to land animals to apes to humans over millions of years. It's amazing how, with all of these scientific and logical minds, they can espouse to theories that defy reasoning and logic. One of the major problems the evolutionists have is what they call "The Missing Link." They cannot explain why, if man evolved from apes, are there still apes today that have not yet evolved. In reality, there is no missing link; their theories are idiotic and unproven. When I was pre-med at Arizona State (age 37) of course I had to take Biology and we studied evolution. I informed my instructor that I did not espouse to this belief but for the sake of my grade I would regurgitate back to him what writers of the book attempted to cram down my throat. One of the teacher's assistants in my Chemistry class told me that the more he learns about Science, the more convinced he was that God did not exist. I looked at him incredulously and said, "Are you kidding me? The more I learn about Science the more positive I am that God truly *does* exist!"

The world we live in and the galaxy in which we turn, could have only been created by a highly intelligent being. The Bible says that, "In the beginning God created the heaven and the earth." (Genesis 1:1) However, this account, just like the plan of salvation, is much too simple for some to grasp. Out of egotistical and prideful hearts, they are unwilling to accept that there could be some being, unseen by their mortal eyes, greater than them. Out of disobedient and hard hearts, they refuse to bow to and give allegiance to an intelligent and holy being who claims to be worthy of worship. They have deceived themselves into believing that they can control their own ultimate destiny; therefore, they have no need of a "judgmental and tyrannical" god who they can't see, hear, smell, taste, or touch. They conclude that he must not exist. However, what they fail to realize is that their minds are finite and temporal. They don't know everything. Even Marilyn vos Savant, with the highest IQ of 223 that has ever been recorded, cannot and never will know everything in these mortal bodies and with these mortal minds.

I used to think I was too smart for God. Of course, I acquired this delusion of grandeur when I first attended college at the age of 17. My head was filled with so many philosophies, theories, and ideologies that there simply wasn't room for God. In addition, God's words and commandments interfered with the kind of life I wanted to live. Therefore, he must and cannot exist. Of course I was not really an atheist; I, too, was a soon-to-be backsliding agnostic. I, along with many people, had been baptized at the age of 9; however, I had no real knowledge of Christ or his sacrifice at Calvary. God knows those that are his; we are predestined and called. (Ephesians 1:5, 11)This is the case even when we do not know who God is, who we are, and even when we are ignorantly serving the Devil by turning our backs on God. God has expert timing. His Holy Spirit knows when and how to draw you. God is our source whether we believe in him or not. Just because we profess disbelief in something does not mean it doesn't exist. We can walk to the edge of a 10-story building and declare with all our might that we don't believe in gravity. However, if we venture off the building, we will come crashing down face-to-face with the reality of gravity.

In the end it comes down to a question of faith. Some professing atheists may claim that they don't have faith in anything. This simply isn't true. They take on faith that if they get into an elevator and push a button, that it will take them to that designated floor. How do they know that by pushing the button it won't trigger a mechanism causing the elevator to go hurtling down to the ground? They take on faith that if they go to their designated place of employment and work for 40 hours that the employer will write them a check for services rendered. Most of all, they take on faith that when they close their eyes at night to go to sleep that they will awake the next morning. One need only examine his or her own body as to how organized and wonderfully-made they are. (Psalm 139:14) Then they can understand that there is no way that it could have been formed by chance. Still there are others who persist in their disbelief. When confronted with a thought-provoking question such as, "What if you're wrong?" they simply shrug and say, "Well, I'll cross that bridge when I come to it." However, I say to you, O' wise and noble one who is a legend in your own mind, consider this: How do you know that the very time you decide you're ready to cross that bridge you painfully discover it is no longer there?

> *Dear God, the enemy continually throws darts of doubt at my faith. I know that I cannot see or feel you with my physical senses, but I put my faith and trust in your word. I know that I am wonderfully and fearfully made. You are omnipotent, omniscient, and omnipresent, and I humble myself in your sight. Amen*

The Pursuit of Happiness

"I know both how to be abased, and I know how to abound: everywhere and in all things I am instructed both to be full and to be hungry, both to abound and to suffer need." Philippians 4:12

It has taken me a long time to find true contentment in my life. It is the type of contentment that allows you to be satisfied and enjoy your earthly existence when your needs are being met and when they're not, when you are being exalted and praised and when you are being humbled and debased, when you're in good health and when you're not, when you're employed and when you're not, when your bills are paid and when your phone rings off the hook from creditors, when you're comfortably protected from the elements in a nice cozy home and when you're homeless, when your belly is full and when it rumbles because you haven't eaten in two days, when you're surrounded by loving family and friends and when you're alone because family and friends are no longer loving, when you're married and when you're single, and when the weather is pleasantly comfortable and when the heat is beating down or the rain, snow, sleet, or hail are causing raging storms all around you. I've experienced all of these and more.

It's easy to complain when things are not going well. However, there is a difference between complaining and explaining. More times than not, we want some other person to whom we can tell our troubles. In fact, this is why psychiatrists and psychologists are so popular. Of course, psychiatrists make a great deal more money because they can prescribe medication while a psychologist cannot. A lot of people who cannot afford either default to their priest, pastor, spouse, support group, best friend, or even their barber, hair stylist, casino card dealer, or bartender. We want someone who we believe cares about us to listen to us and understand us. However, wisdom guides most of us so that we know what to share and to whom to share it. Some people never share their problems with others; they tell no one but God. I had a pastor one time who, whenever I asked him how he was doing, he would say, "Fine." There was a time about a year before he succumbed to cancer when I knew he was not doing well. However, his response was always the same. So, I decided to ask him why he always told me that he was fine even when I knew he was more than likely in pain. He said simply, "Because if it's not fine, it will be."

What a wise man he was. I remember telling the church that this is the type of contentment that I sought in my life. As believers and children of God, we can still have contentment even in the face of impending death because we know the end of our physical lives is not the end of the story. Since physical death is the worst that can happen to us and we know we have eternal life, why do we worry and complain about any less than this? I remember another pastor who is still living who used to always sing a moving and inspirational song that started off, "Though the storms keep raging in my life…" and it would end with, "I won't complain." Complaining about our problems will do nothing to change them. If something can be changed, we need to seek God for direction and guidance, and then roll up our sleeves and get to work. If it cannot be changed, we do best to leave it in God's hands and, like the apostle Paul, who, after petitioning the Lord multiple times to remove his agonizing "thorn in the flesh" with which he was buffeted continually, accepted the Lord's answer with contentment, "My grace is sufficient for you." (2 Corinthians 12:9)

In today's society most people will object to contentment. They say we should always try to make our lives better and that complacency is nothing more than laziness. They are right that one has the right to make his or her life better, but what specifically is "better"? Everyone has to define this for themselves. There is an old adage, "The grass is greener on the other side, but it still has to be mowed." However, contentment and complacency do not mean the same thing. When someone is complacent they are satisfied and pleased with their situation and are unaware that there is some potential danger or defect. People say "ignorance is bliss," however, God is a God of knowledge. The apostle Paul filled his letters with the preface, "Brethren, I would not have you ignorant..." (Romans 1:13; Romans 11:25; 1 Corinthians 10:1; 1 Corinthians 12:1; 2 Corinthians 1:8; 1 Thessalonians 4:13) Contentment is having all of the knowledge of your situation and trusting God in spite of it and knowing that God's will be done. In this is bliss.

There was a story I heard a long time ago that illustrates "creative discontent." There was a young man who was happy and free but he lived in a small one-room mud-thatched house. He always had food to eat, slept on the floor and rode his bike to his place of employment and wherever else he needed to go. Someone took him and showed him a larger house made of adobe with a bedroom and four other rooms. He grew dissatisfied with his one-room abode and worked to acquire the larger house. Since he was farther away from where he worked now, he also bought a vehicle. Now, he was content again. Then someone came and took him and showed him a two-story house with four bedrooms in a neighborhood where people drove newer cars than his and dressed in clothes nicer than his. He soon became dissatisfied with his situation. He demanded more money of his employer. The employer could not afford to pay him more, so he sought out and acquired a job with much higher pay, though it was much more stressful and required much more of his time. However, the man acquired the two-story house, bought a new car and new clothes. Now, he was content again. Then he was invited to a gathering at the home of people who lived in 10 to 15-bedroom mansions, who owned businesses, invested in stock markets, sailed yachts, had private planes, and had more cars and clothes than they could possibly wear in any one lifetime. The man grew seriously discontented and angry. It showed in everything he did and with everyone he met. He demanded more pay of his employer who fired him. Eventually, the man lost everything he had and became homeless and hungry. He found himself staying in shelters and eating at the Mission downtown. His first employer was told of the man's situation. He offered him his old job which he gladly accepted, paid the man's first month's rent on the old one-room mud-thatched house, and bought him another bike so he could get to work each day. The man was again content.

I heard this story many years ago, but doesn't it sound a lot like the Bible's prodigal son? Most of the time we never know and appreciate what we have until it's no longer there. This goes for people, possessions, and situations in our lives. The Bible's word for "happy" is "blessed." It is used 290 times in the King James Version of the Bible. It says that God blessed his people, specific days, and things considered holy. It also says that we were and are blessed by God. Many of the Psalms are filled with words of contentment and thankfulness in spite of life's storms and trials. We are blessed because we do not follow the path of sinners but delight ourselves in God's law by meditating on it day and night. (Psalm 1:1-2) We are blessed because our sin is forgiven and our transgression is covered. (Psalm 32:1) We are blessed because God chose us and allows us to dwell in his courts and to be satisfied in his house which is his holy temple. (Psalm 65:4) We are blessed because God's strength is in us, that we trust in him, that we know the joyful sound, and that we walk in the light of God's countenance. (Psalm 84:5, 12; Psalm 89:15) We are blessed when the Lord chastens us and teaches us out of his law. (Psalm 94:12) We are blessed when we fear the Lord and walk in his ways. (Psalm 128:1)

Our Lord and Savior pronounced numerous blessings upon us in Matthew, chapter 5. He spoke to the hurting and downtrodden. He sought to remind us that happiness comes from humble knowledge that we need God, from having a meek spirit, from having a pure heart, from being a peacemaker, from hungering and thirsting after righteousness, and even from being persecuted for righteousness sake. He assures us that ours is the kingdom of heaven and that we will see God. (Matthew 5:3-12). These promises of contentment and blessings are culminated in the book of Revelation. God assures us through his prophet John that we are blessed for being "called unto the marriage supper of the lamb" (Revelation 19:9), for having "part in the first resurrection: on such the second death hath no power"

(Revelation 20:6), for keeping "the sayings of the prophecy of this book" (Revelation 22:7), and finally, blessed because we "do his commandments" so that we "may have right to the tree of life, and may enter in through the gates into the city" (Revelation 22:14)

> *Dear God, forgive me for murmuring and complaining. Help me to be content with things such as I have and to wait patiently on you to change things in my life that need to be changed. Thank you for your bountiful blessings. Amen*

Recognizing the Counterfeit

"But there were false prophets also among the people, even as there shall be false teachers among you, who privily shall bring in damnable heresies, even denying the Lord that bought them, and bring upon themselves swift destruction." 2 Peter 2:1

Some people think the test of whether or not someone's teachings are true is whether or not that person is truly sincere. However, Jim Jones was sincere; Hitler was sincere; Charles Mason was sincere. They were all sincere, and sincerely wrong. In fact, there are still people, especially young people, today who consider them heroes, try to emulate them, and follow their teachings and terrible acts. Together, they have caused the deception and destruction of thousands of souls who thought they were following the truth. God has true prophets and ministers who speak his truths. There are many false prophets and ministers who speak lies and cause deception. For everything God has that is authentic, the Devil has created a counterfeit. The only way to tell a phony is not by examining the thousands of counterfeits, but by measuring and judging it against the genuine article. This is what bank tellers and representatives do to test whether the $20, $50 or $100 with which they have been presented is authentic or not. By comparison, the only way to judge whether or not a stick is crooked or just how crooked it is, is to place next to it a completely straight stick.

As people of God, the best and only standard of measurement we have for all teachings and behavior is the Bible. Therefore, we must study this standard to know how to rightly divide it, and take care not to take words or verses out of context, thereby avoiding our own private interpretations. (2 Timothy 2:5; 2 Peter 1:20) The Bible in its original text is its own interpreter. We know the word is powerful by the effects it has on people. Paul says, "For the word of God is quick, and powerful, and sharper than any two-edged sword, piercing even to the dividing asunder of soul and spirit, and of the joints and marrow, and is a discerner of the thoughts and intents of the heart." (Hebrews 4:12)

Jesus, who is the expressed written word in bodily form, was the greatest teacher of all and had much to say about false teachings and false teachers. He said that if anyone breaks the least of the commandments and teaches others to follow their lead, will be the least in the Kingdom of Heaven, but those who obey them and teach them will be great in the Kingdom of Heaven. (Matthew 5:19) He called the false teachers "hypocrites" and said they only honor him with their lips but their hearts are far from him. He called their worship a farce because they replace God's commands with their own man-made teachings. (Matthew 15:7-9) Jesus said that not everyone who sounded religious and called out to him, "Lord, Lord," will enter into the Kingdom of Heaven, but he who obeys his Father in heaven. (Matthew 7:21) Jesus truly loved children and he warned that anyone who causes one of the little ones who trust in him to lose faith, it would be better for the person if "a millstone" was "hanged about his neck" and he was "cast into the sea." (Mark 9:42)

Most people are quick to jump on the band wagon. In fact, that is one of advertisers' most popular marketing tools. They tell you everybody who's anybody has one or is doing it. Generally, popularity can be one of the signs of people following false teachings. In a short time, celebrities such as Lady Gaga, Jay-Z, Britney Spears, Beyonce Knowles, and Marilyn Manson have drawn millions and millions of fans, "little monsters" as Lady Gag calls them. Some TV evangelists also draw millions of fans and followers. People have itching ears and want you to tell them they are okay when they sin. They want to believe God approves of what they do. They want to believe that everybody is going to heaven anyway. They want to believe that homosexuality is okay, that it is not a sin, and that they have a right to marry the same sex person and even stand in the pulpit and preach that it is approved by God. Jesus told us that there are much "sorrows that await" those "who are praised by the crowds, for their ancestors also praised false prophets." (Luke 6:26) Jesus also told the people that he was not teaching his own ideas, like those who are looking for praise for themselves, but he was seeking to honor the one who sent him (God) and therefore was teaching the ideas of God. (John 7:16-18)

The apostle Paul had much to say about false teachers. He warned us to watch out for those who cause divisions and upset people's faith by teaching things that are contrary to what the word teaches us. He says such people are seeking their own personal interests and deceive innocent people by their smooth talk and glowing words. (Romans 16:17-18) He urged us not to allow anyone to lead us astray with empty philosophy and high-sounding nonsense that come not from Christ but from human thinking and evil powers of the world. (Colossians 2:6, 8) Paul said some of these teachers burdened the people with ceremonial rules about food, marriage, special days, and man-made requirements, saying "Touch not" or "Handle not" or "Eat not." He says these people are false prophets who believe they will earn special favor with God because of these things. Paul calls them hypocrites and liars who pretend to be religious but their consciences are dead. He reminds us that in the last days there will be those who will no longer listen to right teaching; they will instead follow lying spirits and teachings that come from demons. Paul warns us not to be fooled by them. Lastly, Paul adds that sometimes divisions benefit the body so that false beliefs can be brought into the open so they can be judged. (Colossians 2:20-23; Hebrews 13:9; 2 Corinthians 11:13-15; 1 Timothy 4:1-3; 2 Timothy 6:3-5; 1 Corinthians 11:18-19)

So many church denominations today have embraced the homosexual agenda. It has been accepted and preached, even though the Bible implicitly condemns this behavior and calls it sexual immorality. (Romans 1:18-32) Peter warns of those teaching destructive heresies about God, causing many to follow their evil teaching and shameful immorality. He tells us that those who do so will meet a terrible end because the true way of Christ is slandered. Peter reminds us that God did not spare the angels who followed Lucifer and rebelled against God. He says God is especially hard on those who are proud and arrogant in their rebellion. Peter calls them "unthinking animals, creatures of instinct born to be caught and killed." He says they love to indulge in their evil pleasures in broad daylight; they love to revel in their deceitfulness while they dine with you; they commit adultery with their eyes; their lust is never satisfied, and they make a game of luring unstable people into sin. (2 Peter 2:1-19)

Finally, John cautions us not to believe everyone who claims to speak by the Spirit. We are to test whether or not the spirit they have comes from God because there are many false prophets in the world. If a prophet does not acknowledge Jesus as Lord and Savior, that person is not from God and has the spirit of the Antichrist. Mind you, our Lord and Savior's true name is not Jesus; it is Yahoshua. See the original text of the Bible in Hebrew, Greek, and Aramaic. There was no letter "J" in the Hebrew Language and remains no letter "J" even today. The name "Jew" is a form of the word "Hebrew." So much deception has already occurred as the apostles and Jesus (Yahoshua) predicted. The Spirit of God leads us into all truth even when the enemy tries to hide the truth as he has for so many years. Those who have the spirit of Antichrist, as John says, belong to this world, so the world speaks from the world's viewpoint, and the world listens to them. However, we belong to God and that is why those who know God listen to us. If they do not belong to God, they do not listen to us. John says that this is how we know if someone has the Spirit of truth or the spirit of deception. (1 John 4:1-6)

> *Precious Lord and Savior, sharpen my spiritual radar by the light of truth as revealed in your word. Help me to recognize lies and deception and every false teaching. Give me the courage to uncover those who are false and commend them to your judgment. Thank you for the true teachers of your word.   Amen*

Only One Way Up

"Jesus saith unto him, I am the way, the truth, and the life: no man cometh unto the Father, but by me." John 14:6

Oprah Winfrey is one of the most successful and celebrated Black women of our time since Madame C.J. Walker. She had her own TV talk show for many years, owns her own magazine, should have been nominated for her role as Sophia in the movie, *The Color Purple*, has starred in other films, has produced several TV movies and motion pictures, owns her own television station, operates a school for young girls in Africa, has her own book club, won numerous awards, including The Lifetime Achievement Award, and possibly a host of other accomplishments of which I am unaware. I've written to her six times: a couple of times to request help for other black women and their children, and a couple of times to personally ask for her help with my $130,000 student loan debt. The fifth time I sent her a copy of my novel, *The Last Visitor*, to try to get it included in her book club because I believed it would give me a springboard for book sales. The last time I wrote to her I sent her a synopsis of the book and included my marketing plan. I never heard from her either time. I was very disappointed; however, I still admire her for her achievements.

President Barrack Obama has accomplished something no other Black man with obvious African pigmentation has accomplished: he will forever wear the title of "The First Black President of the United States." Of course there were four black men who were presidents of our colonies before we became the United States, and there have been four presidents of the United States whose blood contained more than the required percentage of African DNA to be classified as "Colored," "Negro," or whatever we were called during their time period. President Obama has a beautiful and intelligent Black wife and two beautiful daughters born to their union. His family gives a whole new meaning to the "White House." He and his wife have been published, he was previously a senator of Chicago, he passed a major healthcare bill, received an honorary Ph.D, was awarded the Nobel Peace Prize, has achieved notoriety and celebrity status in a short time, gave the eulogy at the funeral of Dorothy Heights who helped continue the legacy of the National Council of Negro Women (NCNW), and a host of other achievements of which I am no doubt unaware. I've written to him three times. All three times were to request help with my student loan debt and to witness to him about Christ, and to urge him to become the Black people's champion like he has for Native Americans, big businesses, and homosexuals. Because of the age of my debt, I do not meet all of the requirements that former President Bush set up for loan forgiveness. The last time I wrote to President Obama, I printed in red marker on the back of the envelope: "PLEASE HELP! TEACHER DROWNING IN A SEA OF STUDENT LOANS!" I received a letter on his stationery; whether it was personally from him I'll never know, but the gist of the letter was he understood my problem, he heard me, but in essence, it was my responsibility. I was very disappointed; however, I still admire him for his achievements.

I mention these two because they are household names of Black minorities that have achieved what most people would call "The American Dream." I even saw Shawn Combs, once known as "Puff Daddy," now known as "Diddy," sporting a t-shirt that said, "I Am the American Dream." Of course, there are many other Black minorities who are wealthy and successful, especially athletes, entertainers, and business owners. However, what does a man profit if he "gains the whole world yet lose his own soul?" (Matthew 16:26; Mark 8:36)

How dare I insinuate that these people will lose their souls? Who am I to make such claims? I am absolutely nobody in the world's eyes. However, these are not my claims; they are the Bible's claims; I merely speak the words of truth. I know one day I will have to seal my testimony with my blood, as Jesus has told us. Even so, I do not want anyone to lose their souls or to spend eternity in hell. I don't wish this on my worst enemy, let alone the individuals mentioned above. I want the same thing

God wants: for them to be saved from the wrath to come. Oprah and Obama openly believe homosexuality is not a sin. Obama openly believes abortion is not a sin. Diddy's lifestyle is openly sinful. The operative world is sin: the little three-letter word that will keep most people out of heaven. I believe the word SIN is actually God's acronym that he uses to urgently plead with fallen humanity to "**S**top **I**t **N**ow!" All sin not repented of and not confessed of will result in God's judgment.

There are so many religions in the world that people, including Oprah, profess that "There can't be just one way" to God. However, there is only one true God and his word says that there is only one way to him: through his son, Jesus Christ (Yahoshua). The Bible says, "He that believeth on him is not condemned: but he that believeth not is condemned already, because he hath not believed in the name of the only begotten Son of God." (John 3:18) Then 18 verses later, Jesus repeats it in a different way. When something is repeated it is because the speaker wants to further emphasize the point and to make sure you hear it again in case you missed it the first time. "He that believeth on the Son hath everlasting life: and he that believeth not the Son shall not see life; but the wrath of God abideth on him." (John 3:36)

I used to want to believe that there was more than one way to God because of all the people in the remote places of the earth who have never heard of Jesus. As a teacher, I never hold my students accountable for lessons they never received. However, I've since learned that God will not send people to hell because they did not accept Jesus. He will send them to hell because they have broken the law. Paul reminds us in Romans that, even without the written law, God has given man a conscience to know wrong from right when it comes to dealing with other human beings. Slavery was accepted at one time, but people knew deep inside it was wrong. Some cultures believe it is acceptable to eat another human being. Again, something deep inside them knows it is wrong (possibly the person they ate did not agree with them). In some cultures, they believe that a man infected with AIDS can rid himself of the disease by having sex with a baby; they believe the purity of the child will cure the man. There is something deep inside of them that knows this is terribly wrong. However, people do not truly know how really sinful sin is except by the law. It serves as a schoolmaster to teach us just how far off the mark we really are from God's righteousness.

In addition, these cultures also have their own beliefs with regard to the afterlife. I am a creative person and have found different ways of arriving at an answer or a destination. I always believed that the best way is whatever way is best for you. This works fine on the horizontal plane; however, if one wants to reach the top of a mountain, the only direction and the only way is up. God's kingdom is higher up than the highest mountain. The only way we can get to him is to lift up our heads, believe on the name of the Lord Jesus Christ, and be baptized in his name for the remission of our sins, and receive God's Holy Spirit to seal us unto that day of physical redemption. (Acts 2:38) Of course this belief in Christ involves humbling yourselves at the master's feet and trusting in him to save you as you would a parachute to save you when you have to jump out of an airplane at 10,000 feet – an airplane that has a fire in the engine and is about to crash and burn. The parachute will save the person's life; however, the person will not die because he did not put on the parachute; he will die because he has violated the law of gravity. In other words, if there was no law of gravity, it would not matter whether or not the person put on the parachute. So, failing to put on the parachute is not what destroys him, that is, condemns him. It is God's law of gravity that does this. However, putting on the parachute is the *only way* he will be saved.

Holy Lord, forgive my time of ignorance. Forgive me for failing to acknowledge you as the one and only true God. I denounce all others and I know that Jesus (Yahoshua) is the only way, the truth, and the life. I know that no one can enter the Kingdom of Heaven except through your Son. Thank you, Father Yah, for loving me just that much.   Amen

An Offer of a Lifetime

"Bless the LORD, O my soul, and forget not all his benefits: Who forgiveth all thine iniquities; who healeth all thy diseases; Who redeemeth thy life from destruction; who crowneth thee with lovingkindness and tender mercies; Who satisfieth thy mouth with good things so that thy youth is renewed like the eagle's." Psalm 103:3-5

In today's society of commercialized holidays and other special days, it seems that Halloween and Christmas are the largest revenue-producing times for businesses. In the U.S. alone, Halloween sales bring in over $1 billion. Christmas brings in close to $210 billion. Of course, China makes out like a bandit from the U.S. alone, since we are their biggest importer. China makes over $60 million in exports of Christmas trees and close to $600 million in exports of Christmas tree ornaments to the United States. I don't celebrate Halloween; it is a pagan holiday as is Christmas; however, family members and especially little children do not understand such. There are some things that have nothing to do with salvation, so it is not important to make it an issue of division. However, I notice that during October, Halloween pumpkins and decorations and costumes are in the store aisles, in the yards and rooftops of homes and once-empty commercial lots, and are advertised in the media. Then, on or just after November 1st, the pumpkins are replaced by Christmas trees and stores, homes, and the media advertise toys, gifts, and Christmas decorations. However, more and more, one holiday usually gets lost in the shuffle: Thanksgiving. We do see items displayed for meals to be prepared, but this day is not considered a major money-maker for businesses.

There is a song with lyrics that move the heart of anyone who has been born-again:

"Thank you, Lord
Thank you, Lord
I just want to thank you, Lord.
You've been so good
You've been so good

You've been so good
I just want to thank you, Lord.
You've been my friend
You've been my friend
You've been my friend
I just want to thank you, Lord.
You saved my soul
You saved my soul
You saved my soul
I just want to thank you, Lord."

We have so much for which to be thankful to God that mere words cannot always express our gratitude. My eyes fill with tears of joy "when I think of the goodness of Jesus and all he has done for me. My soul cries out, Hallelujah! Thank God for saving me." There are 150 Psalms written in the Bible: songs with lyrics written to God. No matter how the psalmist starts off the song, it usually culminates in praise and thanksgiving to God, not only for what God has done or will do, but just for who he is. Since no musical scores are provided, the reader has the opportunity to create his or her own music through personal praise and worship with God. Oh, how I love the word of God! Oh, how I love Jesus! I was so inspired by the songs of the Bible writers that over the years I created songs during my own personal worship time with the Lord. The music emanated from a heart of thanksgiving and a heart of love for God's redemption, care, miracles, and provision. Later, the songs reflected my gratitude for God's law, his mercy and grace, and even for his chastening and judgment. Through the work of the Holy Spirit, I published a book called *The Reason Why I Sing*. The songs in the book, like the psalms in the Bible, are lyrics only, for the reader to sing his or her own harmonious praise to God.

I've had to repent several times for words I have spoken aloud expressing my discontent and displeasure with people, to whom we have provided educational services, social services, and counseling, who show gratitude with their lips only. Most of them make promises to volunteer or to give back monetarily; however, most of the time, we never see them again. It's just so hard for me to understand how people can receive so much and give no thought to giving back, not even a small amount. I must confess, however, that there have been a few good, thankful people who have given back through their time and effort. My soul is at peace when I remember that Jesus healed 10 people of leprosy, a disease that turned their entire bodies white and was usually accompanied by sores and boils. This "turning of the skin white" only makes sense when people understand that Hebrews were of African descent and black-skinned. It was believed that leprosy usually came as a judgment from God for some sin that was committed or blasphemous words spoken against God as in the case when Miriam murmured against her brother Moses. (Numbers 12:10) Lepers were pronounced "unclean" and ignorantly treated as outsiders who were to be shunned. They had to live in caves on the outskirts of towns and hide themselves. When others approached, they had to announce they were in the vicinity by calling out "Unclean, unclean!" (Leviticus 13:13-49; Leviticus 14:3-57)

Jesus had compassion on lepers, just as he did on everyone suffering with any kinds of diseases, both physical and spiritual. He healed their infirmities. Though all ten lepers received the gift of healing from our Lord and Savior, only one of them, a Samaritan, turned back to thank Jesus and to give glory to God. Jesus knew that thankfulness is not only for the giver; it is truly for the receiver also: "Were there not ten men who were made clean? Where are the nine? Have not any of them come back to give glory to God, but only this one from a strange land? And he said to him, Get up, and go on your way; your faith has made you well." (Luke 17:17-19) Jesus cast out demonic spirits from many people, forgave their sins, and warned them to sin no more. One such woman from whom he had cast out seven spirits was so grateful that she poured expensive oil on his feet and anointed his feet with her hair. This was out of a heart of love and thanksgiving. Hannah was so grateful to God for fulfilling her earnest long-time prayers for a son, that she gave him, Samuel, back to God for the Lord's service. Giving thanks gives us peace that surpasses all understanding (Philippians 4:7) and "joy unspeakable" (1 Peter 1:8) Our God provides us with so many benefits and gifts that there is no way we can ever repay him. We cannot even out-give him, even when we try. All he wants is for us to accept his free gift of salvation and to be loved, worshipped, and praised for who he is. Sounds to me like the offer of a lifetime.

> *Thank you, Lord. Thank you from the bottom of my heart. I know I can never repay you for all you have done or even will do on my behalf. Let me show others the same love that you have given me to the best of my ability. Let me give back in time, money, and service. I accept your offer. I pray that I can somehow feel deserving of your wonderful grace and mercy. Amen*

Answering the Hard Questions of Our Faith
(Part I)

"But sanctify the Lord God in your hearts: and be ready always to give an answer to every man that asketh you a reason of the hope that is in you with meekness and fear." I Peter 3:15

Sometimes during our witnessing we encounter people who pose questions that are not always easy to answer. In fact, they are questions that we, as believers, have at times pondered ourselves; however, most of us have been afraid to ask them for fear of displaying our ignorance and/or causing others to doubt our walk of faith. Though we can never know everything because God does not reveal everything to us at this time in our earthly lives, we can answer some of the questions to the best of our ability through the word of God. These questions and a great deal of these answers came from *The Way of the Master Evangelism Course* taught by Kirk Cameron and Ray Comfort (www.livingwaters.com)

Why is there suffering? Doesn't this prove there is no loving God?

We live in a fallen creation. The Bible says, "For this reason, as through one man sin came into the world, and death because of sin, and so death came to all men, because all have done evil:" (Romans 5:12). Disease, suffering, and death entered the world as a result of man's sin. So, we shouldn't blame God, but we should blame ourselves. Instead of viewing suffering as an excuse to reject God, suffering should be seen as a very real reason to turn to God. Suffering stands as a terrible testimony to the truth of the explanation given by the word of God. It is sometimes a mystery why God sometimes allows suffering, especially of the innocent; however, despite the mystery, as believers we continue to trust God as did the apostle Paul: "For my strength is made perfect in weakness. Most gladly therefore will I rather glory in my infirmities, that the power of Christ may rest upon me." (I Corinthians 12:9)

What if I'm an atheist and don't believe in your God?

Just because we don't believe in something doesn't make it disappear. If a man walks down a freeway with an 18-wheeler heading toward him, and he says, "I don't believe in traffic," it doesn't change reality. If he does not move out of the way or the truck does not see him in time, which is highly unlikely, the truck will kill him. Also, just because one cannot experience something with our finite and natural senses does not mean it does not exist. The Bible says, "While we look not at the things which are seen, but at the things which are not seen: for the things which are seen are temporal; but the things which are not seen are eternal." (2 Corinthians 4:18) However, if we deal with the things that are seen, we can look at a building and know that there was a builder. The existence of the building itself is absolute proof that there had to be a builder. If we look at a painting, we can know that there was a painter. The existence of the painting itself is absolute proof that there was a painter. In the same way, when we look at creation, we know there is a creator. The existence of creation itself is absolute proof that there is a highly intelligent creator. According to the apostle Paul, there really are no atheists: "For the invisible things of him from the creation of the world are clearly seen, being understood by the things that are made, even his eternal power and Godhead; so that they are without excuse." (Romans 1:20)

What if I don't believe the Bible is God's Word because I believe it was written by men?

When we write a letter to someone, who writes the letter, us or the pen? Of course, we write the letter; the pen is merely the instrument through whom we use to convey our thoughts. In the same way, God is the writer of the Bible; he simply used sanctified, willing, obedient, and fallible men to communicate his thoughts to humanity. It is important to remember that man is fallible as an instrument can be fallible, but God is infallible. Just as we have many different writing instruments in different sizes, shapes, and colors, so too God has many different instruments he uses for different purposes. The Bible says, "For the prophecy came not in old time by the will of man: but holy men of God spake as they were moved by the Holy Ghost." (2 Peter 1:21) In addition, many Bible prophecies, especially those concerning Jesus, have come to pass. One other point to consider is that if the men who wrote the Bible were not inspired and they were lying, why would they include such terrible accounts that reveal their faults, shortcomings, and sins? When people lie, it is usually to cover up wrongdoing and to show them in the best possible light. On the other hand, if they are good men and inspired of God, why would they tell such outlandish lies? King David was a man after God's own heart, yet he committed terrible sins that are revealed for our admonishment. However, he repented and exclaimed, "Behold, thou desirest truth in the inward parts: and in the hidden part thou shalt make me to know wisdom." (Psalm 51:6)

What if I believe that my god is a god of love and forgiveness, and would never send anyone to hell?

This is an example of idolatry, where instead of making a god or idol with our hands, we have created a god within our minds. We have reshaped and remolded the one true God into our own image. We have created a god with whom we can feel more comfortable. We are guilty of breaking part of the second commandment: "Thou shall not make unto thee any graven image, or any likeness of anything that is in heaven above, or that is in the earth beneath, or that is in the water under the earth." (Exodus 20:4) The God of the Bible is holy and just, and will by no means clear the guilty. God is merciful, however, and extends his forgiveness to all who repent and trust in his Son, Jesus Christ (Yahoshua). "Thou shall not bow down thyself to them, nor serve them: for I the LORD thy God am a jealous God, visiting the iniquity of the fathers upon the children unto the third and fourth generation of them that hate me; and showing mercy unto thousands of them that love me, and keep my commandments." (Exodus 20:5)

My God, help me to always trust in you for answers to every concern or question I have as I travel this road of faith. Help me to speak the word in season and out of season. Help me to be ready to give an answer to every man for the reason of my faith. Amen

Answering More Hard Questions of Our Faith
(Part II)

"And unto the angel of the church of the Laodiceans write; These things saith the Amen, the faithful and true witness, the beginning of the creation of God; I know thy works, that thou art neither cold nor hot: I would thou wert cold or hot. So then because thou art lukewarm, and neither cold nor hot, I will spue thee out of my mouth. Because thou sayest, I am rich, and increased with goods, and have need of nothing; and knowest not that thou art wretched, and miserable, and poor, and blind, and naked: I counsel thee to buy of me gold tried in the fire, that thou mayest be rich; and white raiment, that thou mayest be clothed, and that the shame of thy nakedness do not appear; and anoint thine eyes with eyesalve, that thou mayest see. As many as I love, I rebuke and chasten: be zealous therefore, and repent. Behold, I stand at the door, and knock: if any man hear my voice, and open the door, I will come in to him, and will sup with him, and he with me. To him that overcometh will I grant to sit with me in my throne, even as I also overcame, and am set down with my Father in his throne. He that hath an ear, let him hear what the Spirit saith unto the churches."
Revelation 3:14-22

So what if I still cuss, drink, sleep with women and do other things, does that mean I'm not saved?

     A patient may claim that he's healthy but his doctor may think he has a disease. The doctor can see that, despite the protestations of the patient, the patient's face has lost its natural color, that he's lost a considerable amount of weight, and that he's not thinking clearly. The doctor will probably ask the person how his appetite is. A lack of appetite is usually a sign that something isn't right. In the same way, when we come across other people who say they are saved, but all evidence points to the contrary, we probably won't ask them how their prayer life is. Everybody prays. However, we would do well, like the doctor, to ask the person about his appetite, that is, find out if he's hungering and thirsting after the things of God. More specifically, has he been reading his Bible? Someone who isn't right with God will avoid the Scriptures because the word of God brings conviction (knowledge of guilt). Someone once said of the Bible, "This Book will keep me from sin, or sin will keep me from this Book." Remember, one thing Peter did during his thrice denial of Christ was to use cuss words and swear to prove that he had not been with Christ or been taught by him. (Mark 14:71) Remember also the words of Christ himself, "Not everyone that saith unto me, Lord, Lord, shall enter into the kingdom of heaven; but he that doeth the will of my Father which is in heaven." (Matthew 7:21)

So what if I've lied, what if I believe this doesn't make me a bad person?

Usually, a proud, self-righteous person will find it difficult to openly admit his or her sins. During our witnessing and taking a person through a few of the commandments to allow the person to recognize his need and lack of right standing with God, the person may refuse to say at first, "I have lied and that makes me a liar." Sin is like bad breath; it's easy to detect in others, but not so easy to detect in ourselves. So, usually if you turn around and say, "If I told a lie, what would that make me?" Immediately, the person will reply, "A liar." We must remember that the Bible says "lying lips are an abomination to the Lord." (Proverbs 12:22. Even though we may not think there's anything wrong with lying, God says in his word, "But the fearful, and unbelieving, and the abominable, and murderers, and whoremongers, and sorcerers, and idolaters, and all liars, shall have their part in the lake which burneth with fire and brimstone: which is the second death." (Revelation 21:8) Notice that the word includes "all liars." This means even what we call "little white lies."

I've sinned, but what if I confess my sins and say I'm sorry all the time?

This is a common question from people who consider themselves religious such as false converts, Roman Catholics, Muslims, etc., when they are confronted with the fact that they have sinned against God. God is a good, holy, and just judge. When we go to civil court, even though our justice system is imperfect, we would hope that our case is presided over by a good and just judge. A judge will not let a criminal go free just because the person confesses to the crime and says that he or she is sorry and won't do it again. Of course the person should be sorry because the person has broken the law and shouldn't commit the crime again. However, a good judge will demand punishment and/or remuneration, depending on the crime, because justice must be done. So, how much more will God demand that justice is done? He can release us from the requirements of the Law only because someone else (Jesus) took our punishment for us. If we fail to repent, fail to turn from these sins with an intent and fervent heart not to repeat them, and fail to put on the Lord Jesus Christ, we will not escape the wrath to come, no matter how religious we profess we are.

What if I don't agree with anything you're saying and just want" you to do you while I do me?"

When we have presented the truth in love to the best of our ability, and given the erring one everything we can that God has revealed to us and the person puts us a brick wall and refuses to listen, we can leave the person with a few loving reminders before we "shake the dust off our feet." (Mark 6:11; Acts 13:51) Worldwide, there are 150,000 people who die every 24 hours, so we need to get right with God today. In a loving tone, we need to say to the person, "If my eyes meet yours on the Day of Judgment and you are still in your sins, I'm free from your blood because I have told you the truth." This may sound harsh, but what is harsher, that the person would be temporarily offended by our frankness and straightforwardness out of love and concern, or that the person spends eternity in the Lake of Fire? We should never be discouraged. If we have shared the truth, God will be faithful to bring conviction of sin, in his own time. We do well to remember that when Paul shared the gospel with Felix, the governor in Caesarea, and reasoned with him about righteousness, self-control, and judgment, Felix just dismissed Paul. Paul may have thought he made no impact whatsoever; however, the Bible says that "Felix trembled." (Acts

24:25) One plants, one waters, but God gives the increase. (I Corinthians 3:6) God assures us of this through his prophet: "So shall my word be that goeth forth out of my mouth: it shall not return unto me void, but it shall accomplish that which I please, and it shall prosper in the thing whereto I sent it." (Isaiah 55:11)

> *Father in heaven, I renounce today all that is sin. I turn my back on the old person; all things are passed away and behold, all things become new. I have applied your spiritual cosmetics and recommended them to others. I commit my spirit into your hands. I commit my soul into your precious vault of victory. Continue to mold me, test me, and try me in the fire. I am yours forever. Amen*

Alphabetical Index by Topic

Abortion 23
Anger 61
Answering the Hard Questions 180
Answering More Hard Questions 184
Atheism.. 159
Communication with God... 138
Communication with Others...................................... 141
Competition... 94
Contentment... 162
Courage 88
Death.. 27
Demonic Spirits.. 155
Enemies... 128
Envy & Jealousy 82
Evangelism 71
Faith 8
False Teaching 167
Fear.. 64
Forgiveness.. 15
Friendship 113
Generosity... 67
God's Law 80
God's Protection 39
Gossip 106
Grief... 116
Heritage 31
Idolatry... 97
Loneliness.. 109
Lying... 100

Alphabetical In4dex by Topic (cont'd)

Marriage 57

Money 19

Obedience 11

Opportunities 85

Pain & Suffering 77

Patience 34

Perseverance 152

Politics & Government 132

Prophecy 42

Redemption 54

Salvation 171

Self-Control 36

Self-Esteem 148

Sickness 135

Sin & Redemption 74

Spiritual Gifts 144

Suicide 48

Temperance 91

Thankfulness 176

The Bible 45

The Body 103

The Sabbath 123

Work 120

About The Author

E.A. James is a licensed and ordained minister and has been President and Founder of Fast And Indispensable Temporary Help (F.A.I.T.H.) Ministries, Inc., since February, 1999. She is also the Editor-in-Chief of FM Publishing Company. With 10 other colleges (and many student loans), she has a doctorate in Theology & Biblical Counseling (2006), a master's in Education (2004), bachelor's degree in English (1995), and major course work in many other disciplines. Some of these colleges include: Arizona State University, Phoenix Bible College & Seminary, University of Phoenix, University of Southern California, Grand Canyon University, Rio Salado College, Phoenix College, and Ashwood University. E.A. James recognizes that men care about degrees and titles, and therefore, thought it necessary to fulfill this requirement; however, she has come to understand that God (Yahweh) cares nothing about titles and degrees, and that Jesus (Yahoshua) and his disciples were never degreed, yet they preached the word with forthright boldness and through the power of the Spirit of God (Yahweh).

E.A. James says she was born a teacher. She has taught Bible-centered education for 14 years. As a certified teacher in two states, she taught public education for 10 years, Business and Technology for 8 years, and GED classes for 9 years. In addition, the author is a business owner, divorced mother of two adult children who she raised by herself for 20 years. Since 2000, she has owned and operated Geri Lorraine Enterprises, LLC, (www.gerilorraine.org), which provides consulting, business services, education services, and writing and editorial services.

About The Author (cont'd)

E.A. James lived in Coolidge, Arizona most of her younger years and was born in Florence, Arizona. She grew up in the metropolitan L.A. area (Compton, California), and after receiving her call to the ministry in 1987 and fulfilling her obedience to God (Yahweh), she returned to Arizona. It is only since 2010 that she has learned a great deal about her true heritage, roots, and identity to recognize that she is one of the descendants of the Hebrew Israelites who know that the one they called Jesus was really of African descent and whose real name is Yahoshua (Old Testament) and Messiah (New Testament). She says that although she was baptized in the Baptist Church in 1965, she did not really know Yahoshua, what his sacrifice on Calvary meant for her, and the true road to eternal life. She celebrated her rebirth in Yahoshua and accepted him as her Lord and Savior on March 31, 1987.

E.A. James was born Lorraine Juniel. She has published several titles under the name of Lorraine Juniel and has been a freelance writer for 40 years. In 1996 she won the Diamond Homer Trophy for her poem, *Acquired Taste*. The same year she was awarded the $1,000 Poets of the Year Award for *Tears for Molly*. She wrote under the pen name of Elizabeth Abigail James for many years until December 3, 2010, the day she legally changed her name. E.A. James says, through prayer, Yahweh inspired her to change her name to three Biblical names. Her names in Hebrew are: Elisheva (Elizabeth) Avigayil (Abigail) Yaakova (James). She is the author of many other titles which include nonfiction, fiction, poetry, songs, and screenplays. E.A. James says writing, like teaching, is not just something she does; a writer, like a teacher, is what she is.

Book Ordering Information

To order other books by E.A. James or books published by FM Publishing Company, or to inquire about screenplay production rights, go to:

www.fmpublishingcompany.com

www.createspace.com

www.amazon.com

www.ingramSPARKS.com

www.lulu.com

Email: fmpublishing@cox.net

Fax: 800-518-1219

89405215R00108

Made in the USA
Lexington, KY
27 May 2018